WORLD CONFERENCE ON HUMAN RIGHTS

WORLD CONFERENCE ON HUMAN RIGHTS

Editor

Dr. Digumarti Bhaskara Rao
M.Sc., M.A., M.A., M.Ed., Ph.D.
Seccretary
Academy of Communication Culture
Education Science and Service
1-22-10 Srinivasa Nagar
Guntur–522006 (A.P.)

DISCOVERY PUBLISHING HOUSE
NEW DELHI-110002

Reprinted: 2013

ISBN 81-7141-661-6

Published by

DISCOVERY PUBLISHING HOUSE
4831/24, Ansari Road, Prahlad Street,
Darya Ganj, New Delhi-110002 (India)
Phone: 3279245 • Fax: 91-11-3253475
E-mail:dphtemp@indiatimes.com

Printed at:

Dynamic Printers, Delhi

Preface

With the exception of the pursuit of peace, there is no cause with which the United Nations is more closely identified than the cause of human rights. Throughout the world, UN actions in the field of human rights have saved lives, prevented torture, won the release of prisoners, brought about the reappearance of "disappeared" persons, promoted health and literacy and protected the rights of refugees and displaced persons. Provisions of UN treaties have been written into national legislation, affording millions of people the legal basis for claiming respect for their rights. Even when not incorporated into national law, UN standards and the spotlight of UN attention have proven to be powerful tools, curbing abuses and helping restore democratic Governments.

To strengthen this deep commitment to the cause of human dignity, the World Conference on Human Rights took place in Vienna in June 1993, at the invitation of the Government of Austria. The objectives of the Conference were:

- to review and assess progress made in the field of human rights since the adoption of the Universal Declaration of Human Rights in 1948;
- to identify obstacles and ways in which they might be overcome;
- to examine the link between development and the enjoyment of economic, social, cultural, civil and political rights;
- to examine ways to improve the implementation of human rights standards and instruments;

- to evaluate the effectiveness of United Nations methods and mechanisms; and
- to recommend ways to ensure adequate financial and other resources for UN human rights activities.

The conference examined the achievements of the UN human rights programme, evaluated its status and gave it future direction. Particular emphasis was given to achieving universal ratification of basic human rights instruments, promoting human rights education and stepping up technical cooperation programmes to ensure the necessary national infrastructure for promoting and protecting human rights in every country.

The UN Under-Secretary-General for Human Rights, Antoine Blanca (France), was Secretary-General of the Conference. The United Nations Centre for Human Rights was the secretariat for the Conference.

In December 1989, the General Assembly requested the UN Secretary-General to seek the views of Governments, UN agencies and bodies and human rights NGOs as to the desirability of convening a world conference to deal at the highest level with the crucial questions facing the United Nations in the promotion and protection of human rights. The Assembly felt that a world conference could make a major contribution to the effectiveness of the UN and its Member States. The idea received wide support.

On 18 December 1990, the Assembly decided to convene a World Conference. Governments, UN specialised agencies and bodies, international and regional organisations and NGOs were invited to participate in the World Conference and to assist in pre-Conference preparations.

A Preparatory Committee was established, open to all UN Member States or Members of the UN specialized agencies. The Committee was to make proposals to the Assembly on the Conference's agenda, participation and documentation and on preparatory meetings and activities at the international, regional and national levels. Its first session took place in Geneva on 9-13 September 1991, and its second session met in Geneva on 30 March-10 April 1992. The third session was held on 14-18 September 1992, and the fourth in March 1993, both in Geneva.

All countries agreed at the Preparatory Committee that the Conference should not be a meeting of States only, and that NGOs could make an important contribution. Various NGOs have taken part in the Committee's discussions, stating their views on different aspects of the Conference. The World Conference secretariat prepared a number of action-oriented studies and submitted to the fourth session of the Preparatory Committee and to the Conference.

Proposals on the agenda of the Conference have been made by the African Group, the Asian Group, the Latin American and Caribbean Group and the Group of Western European and others States. The UN Commission on Human Rights and several expert bodies have also given their comments.

Regional preparatory meetings were held in 1992 or early 1993 in San José, Costa Rica, for Latin America and the Caribbean; in Bangkok, Thailand, for Asia and the Pacific; and in Tunis, Tunisia, for Africa. In addition, other meetings were also envisaged as part of the preparatory process.

The World Conference on Human Rights took place 25 years after the International Conference on Human Rights, held in Teheran, to mark the International Year for Human Rights and the twentieth anniversary of the Universal Declaration of Human Rights. With the cause of human rights continuing to be at the heart of the international community's search for peace, stability and well-being, the Vienna Conference strengthen UN programmes and inspired renewed international commitment to the cause.

This book on the World Conference on Human Rights present the full original documents of "The Vienna Declaration and Programme of Action" along with the Opening Statement of UN Secretary-General Boutros Boutros-Ghali and the International Bill of Human Rights and Human Rights: A United Nations Priority. I am thankful to the United Nations for reproducing the documents of World Conference on Human Rights, The International Bill of Human Rights and Human Rights; A United Nations Priority.

BHASKARA RAO

Contents

Strengthening Human Rights at the National Level Combating Discrimination

Human Rights and Conflicts

United Nations Landmarks in Human Rights: A Brief Chronology

The Universal Declaration of Human Rights: A Synopsis

International Human Rights Instruments

Office of the United Nations High Commissioner for Human Rights

United Nations Human Rights Monitoring Mechanisms

1

Introduction

The World Conference on Human Rights
Vienna, Austria, 14-25 June 1993

On 25 June 1993, representatives of 171 States adopted by consensus the Vienna Declaration and Programme of Action of the World Conference on Human Rights, thus successfully closing the two-week World Conference and presenting to the international community a common plan for the strengthening of human rights work around the world.

The Conference was marked by an unprecedented degree of participation by government delegates and the international human rights community. Some 7,000 participants, including academics, treaty bodies, national institutions and representatives of more than 800 non-governmental organisations (NGOs)—two thirds of them at the grass-roots level—gathered in Vienna to review and profit from their shared experiences.

United Nations Secretary-General Boutros Boutros-Ghali, in a message to the Conference, told the delegates that by adopting the Vienna Declaration and Plan of Action they had renewed the international community's commitment to the promotion and protection of human rights. He saluted the meeting for having forged "a new vision for global action for human rights into the next century".

The Vienna Declaration and Programme of Action, which is presented in this booklet in its entirety, marks the culmination of a long process of review and debate over the current status of human rights machinery in the world. It also marks the beginning of a renewed effort to strengthen and further implement the body of human rights instruments that have been painstakingly constructed on the foundation of the Universal Declaration of Human Rights since 1948.

In his presentation of the document to the final plenary session, Mr. Ibrahima Fall, the Secretary-General of the Conference, said that the Vienna Declaration provides the international community with a new "framework of planning, dialogue and cooperation" that will enable a holistic approach to promoting human rights and involve actors at all levels—international, national and local.

In 1989 the General Assembly called for the convening of a world meeting that would review and assess progress made in the field of human rights, since the adoption of the Universal Declaration of Human 'Rights, and identify obstacles and ways in which they might be overcome. The first global meeting on human rights had taken place in Teheran in 1968.

In Conference agenda, as set by the forty-seventh session of the General Assembly in 1992, also included the examination of the link between development, democracy and economic, social, cultural, civil and political rights, and the evaluation of the effectiveness of United Nations methods and mechanisms with the aim of recommending ways to ensure adequate financial and other resources for United Nations human rights activities.

From the first of four Preparatory Committee meetings in Geneva in September 1991, it was clear that these were tasks that raised many difficult, sometimes divisive, issues regarding national sovereignty, universality, the role of non-governmental organisations and questions concerning the feasibility, viability and impartiality of new or strengthened human rights instruments.

The search for common ground on these and many other issues was characterised by intense dialogue among Governments and dozens of United Nations bodies, specialised agencies and other intergovernmental organisations and thousands of human rights and development NGOs from around the world.

The preparatory process included three key regional meetings—in Tunis, San José and Bangkok—which produced declarations outlining particular concerns and perspectives of the African, the Latin American and Caribbean and the Asian and Pacific regions. In addition, informal meetings in Europe and North America and scores of satellite meetings throughout the world involving broad spectrums of society made extremely valuable contributions. At the final meeting in May, which ended after an extended session, the Preparatory Committee prepared a draft final document with which the Conference, hosted by the Austrian Government in Vienna, began its work and final negotiations.

The final document agreed to in Vienna, which was endorsed by the forty-eighth session of the General Assembly (resolution 48/121, of 1993), reaffirms the principles that have evolved during the past 45 years and further strengthens the foundation for additional progress in the area of human rights. The recognition of the interdependence between democracy, development and human rights, for example, prepares the way for future cooperation by international organisations and national agencies in the promotion of all human rights, including the right to development.

Similarly, the Conference took historic new steps to promote and protect the rights of women, children and indigenous peoples by, respectively, supporting the creation of a new mechanism, a Special Rapporteur on Violence against Women; calling for the universal ratification of the Convention on the Rights of the Child by the year 1995; and recommending the proclamation by the General Assembly of an international decade of the world's indigenous peoples. Subsequently, the General Assembly carried out that recommendation.

The Vienna Declaration also makes concrete recommendations for strengthening and harmonizing the monitoring capacity of the United Nations system. In this regard, it called for the establishment of a Higher Commissioner for Human Rights by the General Assembly, which subsequently created the post on 20 December 1993 (Resolution 48/141). Mr. José Ayala Lasso was nominated by the Secretary-General as the first High Commissioner and assumed office on 5 April 1994.

The Vienna Declaration further emphasises the need for speedy ratification of other human rights instruments and for additional resources for the Centre for Human Rights, which served as the secretariat of the World Conference.

"In adopting this Declaration", Mr. Fall concluded in his final address to the Conference, "the Member States of the United Nations have solemnly pledged to respect human rights and fundamental freedoms and to undertake individually and collectively actions and programmes to make the enjoyment of human rights a reality for every human being."

In addition to the text of the Vienna Declaration and Programme of Action, this book features the opening address to the World Conference of Secretary-General Boutros Boutros-Ghali on 14 June, in which he describes the historical context of the first global meeting on human rights in 25 years and the pressing needs which the final document would have to address.

2

Human Rights The Common Language of Humanity

The following is the text of the statement made by Secretary-General Boutros Boutros-Ghali in Vienna at the opening of the World Conference on Human Rights on 14 June 1993.

The World Conference on Human Rights being convened today at Vienna marks one of those rare, defining moments when the entire community of States finds itself under the gaze of the world.

It is the gaze of the billions of men and women who yearn to recognise themselves in the discussions that we shall be conducting and the decisions that we shall be taking in their name. It is the gaze of all those men and women who, even now, are suffering in body and spirit because their human dignity is not recognised, or is being flouted. It is the gaze of history, as we meet at this crucial juncture.

When in 1989 the United Nations General Assembly requested the Secretary-General to seek the views of Governments and the organisations concerned on the desirability of convening a world conference on human rights, it was demonstrating remarkable historical intuition.

Two months earlier, the Berlin Wall had fallen, carrying away with it a certain vision of the world, and thereby opening up new perspectives. It was in the name of freedom, democracy and human rights that entire peoples were speaking out. Their determination, their abnegation—sometimes their sacrifices—reflected then, and still reflect, their commitment to do away with alienation and totalitarianism.

Thus preparations for today's Conference have gone hand in hand with an impressive acceleration of the course of history.

That conjunction of events must not be seen as pure chance or mere coincidence. It is always when the world is undergoing a metamorphosis, when certainties are collapsing, when the lines are becoming blurred, that there is greatest recourse to fundamental reference points, that the quest for ethics becomes more urgent, that the will to achieve self-understanding becomes imperative.

It is therefore natural that the international community should today feel the need to focus on its own values and, reflecting on its history, ask itself what constitutes its innermost identity—in other words, ask questions about humanity and about how, by protecting humanity, it protects itself.

The goals of the Conference faithfully reflect the following key questions:

What progress has been made in the field of human rights since the Universal Declaration of 1948?

What are the obstacles and how are they to be overcome?

How can implementation of the human rights instruments be enhanced?

How effective are the methods and mechanisms established by the United Nations?

What financial resources should be allocated for United Nations action to promote human rights?

And, at a deeper level, what are the links between the goals pursued by the United Nations and human rights, including the link between development and the enjoyment of economic, social, cultural, civil and political rights?

These are universal questions, but there is no single answer to any of them. While human rights are common to all members of the international community, and each member of that community recognises himself in them, each cultural epoch has its own special way of helping to implement them. In this connection, a debt of thanks is owed to Member States which, at the regional level, have reminded others of this reality.

Yet this reminder must be a source of positive reflection, not of sterile misunderstanding.

Indeed human rights, viewed at the universal level, bring us face-to-face with the most challenging dialectical conflict ever: between "identity" and "otherness", between the "myself" and "others". They teach us in a direct, straightforward manner that we are at the same time identical and different.

Thus the human rights that we proclaim and seek to safeguard can be brought about only if we transcend ourselves, only if we make a conscious effort to find our common essence beyond our apparent divisions, our temporary differences, our ideological and cultural barriers.

In sum, what I mean to say, with all solemnity, is that the human rights we are about to discuss here at Vienna are not the lowest common denominator among all nations, but rather what I should like to describe as the "irreducible human element", in other words, the quintessential values through which we affirm together that we are a single human community.

I do not want to underestimate the nature of our undertaking. Yet in such an area, this is no time seek cautious compromise or approximate solutions, to be content with soothing declarations, or, worse still, to become bogged down in verbal battles. On the contrary, we must ascend to a conception of human rights that would make such rights truly universal!

There lies the challenge of our endeavour; there lies our work; there stands or falls this Conference in future evaluations.

An awareness of the complexities of the debate is the first step towards developing a method of debate. We should be under no illusion: a debate on human rights involves complex issues. Human rights should be viewed not only as the absolute yardstick which they are, but also as a synthesis resulting from a long historical process.

As an absolute yardstick, human rights constitute the common language of humanity. Adopting this language allows all peoples to understand others and to be the authors of their own history. Human rights, by definition, are the ultimate norm of all politics.

As an historical synthesis, human rights are, in their essence, in constant movement. By that I mean that human rights have a dual nature. They should express absolute timeless injunctions, yet simultaneously reflect a moment in the development of history. Human rights are both absolute and historically defined.

The reason I began with these statements of principle—at the risk of appearing very abstract—is that I am convinced that there will be no appropriate solutions to any of the issues that we shall be considering in the coming days, even the most technical unless we bear in mind the fundamental dialectical conflict between the universal and the particular, between identity and difference.

What makes our task especially urgent is the fact that with the development of communications, every day the whole world is called to witness the free enjoyment—or the violation—of human rights.

Not a day goes by without scenes of warfare or famine, arbitrary arrest, torture, rape, murder, expulsion, transfers of population, and ethnic cleansing. Not a day goes by without reports of attacks on the most fundamental freedoms. Not a day goes by without reminders of racism and the crimes it spawns, intolerance and the excesses it breeds, underdevelopment and the ravages it causes.

And what confronts those men, women and children who are suffering and dying is a reality that is more unbearable than ever; we are all similar yet history emphasises our differences and separates us on all sorts of grounds; political, economic, social and cultural.

We have indeed learned that it is possible to view differences as such with respect, as sources of mutual enrichment; yet when differences become synonymous with inequalities, they cannot but be perceived a unjust. Today, all peoples and all nations share these feelings. That fact in itself is a step forward in the conscience of humanity.

The more so since to move from identifying inequality to rebelling against injustice is only possible in the context of a universal affirmation of the idea of human rights. Ultimately, it is this idea which allows us to move from ethical to legal considerations, and to impose value judgements and juridical norms on human activity.

Let us not delude ourselves, however. Because judgements are based on this scale of constraints and values, it is also part of the power stakes. No doubt this is why some States seek—often and by various means—to appropriate human rights for their own benefit, even turning them into a instrument of national policy. There is no denying that some States constantly try to hijack or confiscate human rights.

Of course in saying this, I do not mean to point a finger at any member of the international community. I only want to stress that human rights, in their very expression, reflect a power relationship.

Let us be clear about this. Human rights are closely related to the way in which States consider them; in other words, to the ways in which States govern their people; them; in yet other words, to the level of democracy in their political regimes.

If we bear all these problems in mind, I am positive that we shall avert the dual danger lurking ahead of us at the outset of this Conference: the danger of a cynical approach according to which the international dimension of human rights is nothing more than an ideological cover for the *realpolitik* of

States; and the danger of a naive approach according to which human rights would be the expression of universally shared values towards which all the members of the international community would naturally aspire.

These considerations should remain present in our minds throughout our discussions, so that we might be bold in our proposals and firm in our principles.

In this regard, I should like to issue a solemn call: that this Conference should measure up to the subject matter and that it should be guided by a threefold requirement, which I shall refer to as "the three imperatives of the Vienna Conference": universality, guarantees, democratization.

Let us deal first with the imperative of universality. To be sure, human rights are a product of history. As such, they should be in accordance with history, should evolve simultaneously with history and should give the various peoples and nations a reflection of themselves that they recognise as their own. Yet, the fact that human rights keep pace with the course of history should not change what constitutes their very essence, namely their universality.

Secondly, there is the imperative of guarantees. Every day we see how discredited human rights and the United Nations itself would be, in the eyes of the world, if the declarations, covenants, charters, conventions and treaties that we draft in order to protect human rights remained dead letters or were constantly violated. Human rights should therefore be covered by effective mechanisms and procedures to guarantee and protect them and to provide sanctions.

Lastly, there is the imperative of democratization. In my opinion, this is essentially what is at stake as we approach the end of the century. Only democracy, within States and within the community of States, can truly guarantee human rights. It is through democracy that individual rights and collective rights, the rights of peoples and the rights of persons, are reconciled. It is through democracy that the rights of States and rights of the community of States are reconciled.

It is on those three imperatives—universality, guarantees

and democratization—that I should like you to reflect.

The imperative of universality will undoubtedly be in evidence throughout our debates. How could it be otherwise? Universality is inherent in human rights. The Charter is categorical on this score: Article 55 states that the United Nations shall promote "universal respect for, and observance of, human rights and fundamental freedoms for all without distinction as to race, sex, language, or religion". The title of the 1948 Declaration—universal, not international—reinforces this perspective.

However, this concept of universality must also be clearly understood and accepted by everyone. It would be a contradiction in terms if this imperative of universality on which our common conception of human rights is based were to become a source of misunderstanding among us.

It must therefore be stated, in the clearest possible terms, that universality is not something that is decreed, nor is it the expression of the ideological domination of one group of States over the rest of the world.

By its nature and composition, it is the General Assembly of the United Nations that is best equipped to express this idea of universality, and we should pay tribute to the human rights standard-setting in which it has been engaged for almost 50 years now.

As a result of its activities, the areas of protection have become increasingly precise: punishment of genocide, suppression of genocide, abolition of slavery, efforts to combat torture and to eliminate all forms of discrimination based on race, sex, religion or belief.

Moreover, the subjects of those rights have been more clearly defined: right of peoples; protection of refugees, stateless persons, women, children, disabled persons, persons with mental illness, prisoners, victims of enforced disappearance; protection of the rights of migrant workers and their families; and protection of indigenous people. In this connection, the General Assembly is to be commended for drafting, as part of the activities relating to the International Year of the World's Indigenous People, a universal declaration for consideration next autumn.

The set of instruments resulting from this standard-setting by the United Nations General Assembly is now our common property. It has enough to satisfy all States, all peoples and all cultures, for the universality it affirms is that of the international community as a whole.

If we look closely at these instruments, and the World Conference on Human Rights affords an ideal opportunity to do so, we may be struck by, and justifiably proud of, the ceaseless efforts made by the General Assembly to develop on the very idea of universality.

While a general, abstract concept of human rights, born of liberal values, prevailed initially, as we can see from the text of the 1948 Universal Declaration, the input of the socialist States and the States of the third world helped broaden this initial vision. The 1966 Covenants bear witness to the broadening of our vision. They enable us to affirm, and I wish to emphasise this here, that civil and political rights and economic, social and cultural rights are equally important and worthy of attention.

We all know, however, that the General Assembly did not stop there: it expanded still further on the concept of universality by enunciating, after these collective rights, what I like to call rights of solidarity, rights which bring us back to a projected universality involving the joint action of all members of society both nationally and internationally. Since Article 1 of the Charter enunciated the right of peoples to self-determination, the General Assembly has proclaimed the right to a healthy environment, the right to peace, the right to food security, the right to ownership of the common heritage of mankind and, above all, the right to development.

I believe that this last right, in particular, shows just how modern the concept of universality is. The General Assembly went a long way towards recognizing this when, as early as 1979, it asserted that "the right to development is a human right" and that "equality of opportunity for devolvement is a prerogative both of nations and of individuals who make up nations".

This idea was expressed when more clearly when, in 1986, the Assembly adopted a Declaration on the Right to Development which states that "the human person is the central subject of development and should be the active participant and beneficiary of the right to development". In that same instrument, the Assembly emphasises the corresponding duties which this right imposes on States: the duty to cooperate with each other in ensuring development, the duty to formulate international development policies and, at the national level, the duty to ensure "access to basic resources, education, health services, food, housing, employment and the fair distribution of income".

I think that this approach to the concept of universality is the right one and that it is this course that we should follow.

We must recognise that while ideological splits and economic disparities may continue to be the hallmark of our international society, they cannot interfere with the universality of human rights.

I believe that at this moment in time it is less urgent to define new rights than to persuade States to adopt existing instruments and apply them effectively.

I also believe that regional organisations have a positive role to play in making States increasingly aware of this problem. Regional action for the promotion of human rights in no way conflicts with United Nations action at the universal level—quite the opposite.

I understand the recent regional meetings on human rights as reflecting a concern to remain true to this concept of universality, no matter what serious problems or legitimate questions it may raise.

The imperative of guarantees should be the second

concern of our Conference. What do human rights amount to without suitable machinery and structures to ensure their effectiveness, both internally and internationally? Here again, the Vienna Conference must not lapse into unproductive debates or futile polemics. To avoid this, the Conference must go back to the very essence of human rights in international society, and to what is unique about them.

I am tempted to say that human rights, by their very nature, do away with the distinction traditionally drawn between the internal order and the international order. Human rights give rise to a new legal permeability. They should thus not be considered either from the viewpoint of absolute sovereignty or from the viewpoint of political intervention. On the contrary, it is must be understood that human rights call for cooperation and coordination between States and international organisations.

In this context, the State should be the best guarantor of human rights. It is the State that the international community should principally entrust with ensuring the protection of individuals.

However, the issue of international action must be raised when States prove unworthy of this task, when they violate the fundamental principles laid down in the Charter of the United Nations, and when—far from being protectors of individuals—they become tormentors.

For us, this problem is a constant challenge, particularly since the flow of information and the effect of world public opinion make the issues in question even more pressing.

In these circumstances, the international community must take over from the States that fail to fulfil their obligations. This is a legal and institutional construction that has nothing shocking about it and does not, in my view, harm our contemporary notion of sovereignty. For I am asking—I am asking us—whether a State has the right to expect absolute respect from the international community when it is tarnishing the noble concept of sovereignty by openly putting that concept to a use that is rejected by the conscience of the world and by the law. Where sovereignty becomes the ultimate argument put forward by authoritarian regimes to support their undermining of the rights and freedoms of men, women and children, such sovereignty—and I state this as a sober truth—is already condemned by history.

Moreover, I believe all members of the international community have an interest in international action being thus defined and directed. Nothing would be more detrimental to States themselves than to leave private agencies or non-governmental organisations to take sole responsibility for protecting human rights in individual States.

Yes, States must be convinced that the control exercised by the international community ultimately results in the greatest respect for their sovereignty and spheres of competence.

The Vienna Conference has therefore rightly decided to evaluate methods and machinery for guaranteeing human rights with a view to improving them. It is indeed important that all of us here be aware of the changes that have taken place, where such forms of control are concerned, at the administrative and jurisdictional levels and in the operational sphere.

At the administrative level, the number of procedures for guaranteeing human rights has been increasing for years, not only within the United Nations, but also at such specialised agencies as the International Labour Organisation (ILO) and the United Nations Educational, Scientific and Cultural Organisation (UNESCO) and at such regional organisations as the Council of Europe and the Organisation of American States.

Within the United Nations, and proliferation of bodies each entrusted with monitoring implementation of a specific convention can even be noted.

At a more general level, the Commission on Human Rights and the United Nations Centre for Human Rights must be accorded a special place.

The Centre, in particular, has undergone profound changes in recent years.

Initially designed to carry out studies and provide information on all aspects of human rights, the Centre has gradually been called on to contribute to the implementation of conventions, and to participate in ad hoc committees of special rapporteurs set up to investigate such wide-ranging matters as summary executions, disappearances and instances of arbitrary detention.

However, guaranteeing human rights also means setting up jurisdictional controls to punish any violations that occur.

In this area, regional organisations have shown the way—particularly in the context of the Council for Europe, in the form of the European Court of Human Rights, and in the Americas, in the form of the Inter-American Court.

I would draw your attention in this connection to the current efforts by the United Nations to promote both a permanent international criminal court and a special international tribunal to prosecute the crimes committed in the former Yugoslavia.

It was in February of this year that the Security Council decided to establish such a tribunal "for the prosecution of persons responsible for serious violations of international humanitarian law committed in the territory of the former Yugoslavia since 1991".

In asking the Secretary-General to consider this project, the Security Council has given itself an entirely new mandate. On 27 May, the Tribunal was established by a unanimous decision of the Security Council, acting under Chapter VII of the Charter. This method has the advantage of giving immediate effect to the establishment of the Tribunal, since all States are required to take the necessary steps to implement a decision adopted in this manner. The Council has thus created, in the context of an enforcement measure, a subsidiary organ as envisaged in Article 29 of the Charter, but one of a judcial nature.

I cannot discuss the development of measures taken by the Organisation to safeguard human rights without mentioning the decisive action taken by the General Assembly in the area of humanitarian assistance.

Since December 1988, when the General Assembly adopted resolution 43/131 on humanitarian assistance to victims of natural disasters and similar emergency situations, the notion of a right to humanitarian assistance has, to a certain extent, become one of the areas in which human rights can actually be guaranteed.

We have seen this reflected in the Organisation's operations in the Sudan, in Somalia, in the special case of Iraq and, today, in the former Yugoslavia.

Once again, these resolutions are not intended to justify some ostensible right of intervention, but simply to reflect one of the key ideas lying behind current efforts to safeguard human rights: the relationship between such guarantees and the imperative of democratisation which the international community is rightly embracing today.

The imperative of democratisation is the last—and surely the most important—rule of conduct which should guide our work. There is a growing awareness of this imperative within the international community. The process of democratisation cannot be separated, in my view, from the protection of human rights. More precisely, democracy is the political framework in which human rights can best be safeguarded.

This is not merely a statement of principle, even less a concession to a fashion of the moment, but the realisation that a democracy is the political system which best allows for the free exercise of individual rights. It is not possible to separate the United Nations promotion of human rights from the establishment of democratic systems within the international community.

Let me not be misunderstood nor unwittingly cause offence.

When, like so many others before me, I stress the imperative of democratization, I do not mean that some States should imitate others slavishly, nor do I expect them to borrow political system that are alien to them, much less try to gratify certain Western States—in fact, just the opposite. Let us state, forcefully, that democracy is the private domain of on one. It can and ought to be assimilated by all cultures. It can take many forms in order to accommodate local realities more effectively. Democracy is not a model to copy from certain States, but a goal to be achieved by all peoples! It is the political expression of our common heritage. It is something to be shared by all. Thus, like human rights, democracy has a universal dimension.

To avoid misinterpretations and misunderstandings, we must all agree that democratisation must not be a source of concern to some but should be an inspiration for all States. In this spirit the United Nations, in its mission to guarantee human rights, has an obligation to help States—often those that are the most disadvantaged—along the ever difficult road to democratization.

This is why we must distance ourselves from sterile polemics and act constructively to build the link effectively between democracy, development and human rights, a link we already recognise as inescapable.

On thing is certain: there can be no sustainable development without promoting democracy and, thus, without respect for human rights. We all know that, on occasion, undemocratic practices and authoritarian policies have marked the first steps taken by some countries along the road to development. Yet, we also know that if these States do not undertake democratic reforms once they have begun to experience economic progress, they will ultimately achieve nothing more than disembodied growth, a source of greater inequity and, eventually, social unrest. Democracy alone can given development its true meaning.

This analysis must lead the developed countries to take an increasingly responsible attitude *vis-a-vis* States that are engaged in the democratisation process. More than ever before, each one must realise its own responsibility in what is a joint undertaking. Each one must understand that development assistance contributes to the promotion of democracy and human rights. This in no way diminishes the overriding responsibility of all States, including the developing countries, to promote democracy and human rights at home. This matter is of concern to the entire international community, for only through individual development can peace for all be ensured.

Each passing day shows that authoritarian regimes are potential causes of war and of the extent to which, conversely, democracy is a guarantor of peace. We have only to look at the mandates given to the United Nations forces to see the connection which the Organisation is making, at the operational level and in the most concrete terms possible, between peace-keeping, the establishment of democracy and the safeguarding of human rights.

The mandate given to the United Nations operation in Namibia from April 1989 to March 1990 was an early but powerful demonstration of this evolution. Since 1991, a number of major operations have incorporated this political dimension—the safeguarding of human rights and the restoration of democracy—in their mission. We have seen this in the operations in Angola, Mozambique, El Salvador, Somalia and, of course, Cambodia.

Many States, in fact, know full well how desirable it is to receive the electoral assistance which they are requesting with increasing frequency from the United Nations.

In 1989, a mission was set up to monitor the electoral process in Nicaragua. The following year, a similar mission was set up in Haiti. Requests for electoral assistance continued to increase at a steady rate, and in the autumn of 1991 the General Assembly endorsed the creation, within the Department of Political Affairs, on an electoral assistance unit, which became operational in April 1992.

Since then, equipped with this new tool, the United Nations has been better able to meet the requests for electoral assistance from many States: Argentina, Burundi, Central African Republic, Chad, Colombia, Congo, Djibouti, Equatorial Guinea, Eritrea, Ethiopia, Guinea, Guinea-Bissau, Guyana, Kenya, Lesotho, Madagascar, Malawi, Mali, Niger, Rwanda, Romania, Senegal Seychelles, Togo, Uganda... the list is impressive.

Such requests fall into a variety of categories: the organisation and holding of elections, their monitoring and verification, on-site coordination of international observers and with the many forms of technical assistance required for democratic elections to take place smoothly.

This a major undertaking for the United Nations, and one whose magnitude must be stressed. The supervision and monitoring of elections do not in themselves constitute long-term guarantees of democratisation and respect for human rights. This is borne out, unfortunately, by the experiences of Angola and Haiti. The United Nations cannot guarantee that there will be enough of a sense of democracy for election results to be respected.

And so we have to do even more. We must help States change attitudes, convince them to undertake structural reforms. The United Nations must be able to provide them with technical assistance that will allow them to adapt their institutions, educate their citisens, train leaders and set up regulatory mechanisms that respect democracy and reflect a concern for human rights. I am thinking specifically of how important it is to create independent systems for the administration of justice, to establish armies that respect the rule of law, to create a police force that safeguards public freedoms, and to set up systems for educating the population in human rights.

It is my conviction that our task is nothing less than setting up a civics workshop on a global scale.

Only by heightening the international community's awareness of human rights in this way and involving everyone in this effort can we prevent future violations that our conscience, and the law, will condemn. Here, as elsewhere, preventive diplomacy is urgently needed.

I look to the Conference to offer suggestions, innovations and proposals to give increasing substance to this human rights diplomacy.

Through these thoughts and illustrations I hope that I have shown that the United Nations has taken a decisive turn in its history. Imperceptibly, our determination to respect human rights is now beginning to be reflected, through concrete and pragmatic efforts, in everything we do.

This has been an important lesson for us which we must bear in mind throughout this Conference: the safeguarding of human rights is both a specific and a general goal. On the one hand, it requires us to identify increasingly specific rights and to imagine increasingly effective guarantees. But it also shows us that human rights permeate all activities of our Organisation, of which they are, simultaneously, the very foundation and the supreme goal.

Allow me, then, by way of conclusion and at the outset of this Conference to make a final appeal:

May human rights create for us here a special climate of solidarity and responsibility!

May they serve to bind the Assembly of States and the human community!

And, finally, may human rights become the common language of all humanity!

3

The Vienna Declaration and Programme of Action

Adopted on 25 June 1993 by the World Conference on Human Rights

The World Conference on Human Rights,

Considering that the promotion and protection of human rights is a matter of priority for the international community, and that the Conference affords a unique opportunity to carry out a comprehensive analysis of the international human rights system and of the machinery for the protection of human rights, in order to enhance and thus promote a fuller observance of those rights, in a just and balanced manner,

Recognizing and affirming that all human rights derive from the dignity and worth inherent in the human person, and that the human person is the central subject of human rights and fundamental freedoms, and consequently should be the principal beneficiary and should participate actively in the realisation of these rights and freedoms,

Reaffirming their commitment to the purposes and principles contained in the Charter of the United Nations and the Universal Declaration of Human Rights,

Reaffirming the commitment contained in Article 56 of the Charter of the United Nations to take joint and separate action, placing proper emphasis on developing effective international cooperation for the realisation of the purposes set out in Article 55, including universal respect for, and observance of human rights and fundamental freedoms for all,

Emphasizing the responsibilities of all States, in conformity with the Charter of the United Nations, to develop and encourage respect for human rights and fundamental freedoms for all, without distinction as to race, sex, language or religion,

Recalling the Preamble to the Charter of the United Nations, in particular the determination to reaffirm faith in fundamental human rights, in the dignity and worth of the human person, and in the equal rights of men and women and of nations large and small,

Recalling also the determination expressed in the Preamble of the Charter of the United Nations to save succeeding generations from the scourge of war, to establish conditions under which justice and respect for obligations arising from treaties and other sources of international law can be maintained, to promote social progress and better standards of life in larger freedom, to practice tolerance and good neighbourliness, and to employ international machinery for the promotion of the economic and social advancement of all peoples,

Emphasizing that the Universal Declaration of Human Rights, which constitutes a common standard of achievement for all peoples and all nations, is the source of inspiration and has been the basis for the United Nations in making advances in standard setting as contained in the existing international human rights instruments, in particular the International Covenant on Civil and political Rights and the International Covenant on Economic, Social and Cultural Rights,

Considering the major changes taking place on the international scene and the aspirations of all the peoples for an international order based on the principles enshrined in the Charter of the United Nations, including promoting and encouraging respect for human rights and fundamental freedoms for all and respect for the principle of equal rights and self-determination of peoples, peace, democracy, justice, equality, rule of law, pluralism, development, better standards of living and solidarity,

Deeply concerned by various forms of discrimination and violence, to which women continue to be exposed all over the world,

Recognizing that the activities of the United Nations in the field of human rights should be rationalised and enhanced in order to strengthen the United Nations machinery in this field and to further the objectives of universal respect for observance of international human rights standards,

Having taken into account the Declarations adopted by the three regional meetings at Tunis, San José and Bangkok and the contributions made by Governments, and bearing in mind the suggestions made by intergovernmental and non-governmental organisations, as well as the studies prepared by independent experts during the preparatory process leading to the World Conference on Human Rights,

Welcoming the International Yeaı of the World's Indigenous People 1993 as a reaffirmation of the commitment of the international community to ensure their enjoyment of all human rights and fundamental freedoms and to respect the value and diversity of their cultures and identities,

Recognizing also that the international community should devise ways and means to remove the current obstacles and meet challenges to the full realisation of all human rights and to prevent the continuation of human rights violations resulting thereof throughout the world,

Invoking the spirit of our age and the realities of our time which call upon the peoples of the world and all States Members of the United Nations to rededicate themselves to the global task of promoting and protecting all human rights and fundamental freedoms so as to secure full and universal enjoyment of these rights,

Determined to take new steps forward in the commitment of the international community with a view to achieving substantial progress in human rights endeavours by an increased and sustained effort of international cooperation and solidarity,

Solemnly adopts the Vienna Declaration and programme of Action.

I

1. The World Conference on Human Rights reaffirms the solemn commitment of all States to fulfil their obligations to promote universal respect for, and observance and protection of, all human rights and fundamental freedoms for all in accordance with the Charter of the United Nations, other instruments relating to human rights, and international law. The universal nature of these rights and freedoms is beyond question.

In this framework, enhancement of international cooperation in the field of human rights is essential for the full achievement of the purposes of the United Nations.

Human rights and fundamental freedoms are the birthright of all human beings; their protection and promotion is the first responsibility of Governments.

2. All peoples have the right of self-determination. By virtue of that right they freely determine their political status, and freely pursue their economic, social and cultural development.

Taking into account the particular situation of peoples under colonial or other forms of alien domination or foreign occupation, the World Conference on Human Rights recognises the right of peoples to take any legitimate action, in accordance with the Charter of the United Nations, to realise their inalienable right of self-determination. The World Conference on Human Rights considers the denial of the right of self-determination as a violation of human rights and underlines the importance of the effective realisation of this right.

In accordance with the Declaration on Principles of International Law concerning Friendly Relations and Cooperation Among States in accordance with the Charter of the United Nations, this shall not be construed as authorizing or encouraging any action which would dismember or impair, totally or in part, the territorial integrity or political unity of sovereign and independent States conducting themselves in compliance with the principle of equal rights and self-determination of peoples and thus possessed of a Government representing the whole people belonging to the territory without distinction of any kind.

3. Effective international measures to guarantee and monitor the implementation of human rights standards should be taken in respect of people under foreign occupation, and effective legal protection against the violation of their human rights should be provided, in accordance with human rights norms and international law, particularly the Geneva Convention relative to the Protection of Civilian Persons in Time of War, of 14 August 1949, and other applicable norms of humanitarian law.

4. The promotion and protection of all human rights and fundamental freedoms must be considered as a priority objective of the United Nations in accordance with its purposes and principles, in particular the purpose of international cooperation. In the framework of these purposes and principles, the promotion and protection of all human rights is a legitimate concern of the international community. The organs and specialised agencies related to human rights should therefore further enhance the coordination of their activities based on the consistent and objective application of international human rights instruments.

5. All human rights are universal, indivisible and interdependent and interrelated. The international community must treat human rights globally in a fair and equal manner, on the same footing, and with the

same emphasis. While the significance of national and regional particularities and various historical, cultural and religious backgrounds must be borne in mind, it is the duty of States, regardless of their political, economic and cultural systems, to promote and protect all human rights and fundamental freedoms.

6. The efforts of the United Nations system towards the universal respect for, and observance of, human rights and fundamental freedoms for all, contribute to the stability and well-being necessary for peaceful and friendly relations among nations, and to improved conditions for peace and security as well as social and economic development, in conformity with the Charter of the United Nations.

7. The processes of promoting and protecting human rights should be conducted in conformity with the purposes and principles of the Charter of the United Nations, and international law.

8. Democracy, development and respect for human rights and fundamental freedoms are interdependent and mutually reinforcing. Democracy is based on the freely expressed will of the people to determine their own political, economic, social and cultural systems and their full participation in all aspects of their lives. In the context of the above, the promotion and protection of human rights and fundamental freedoms at the national and international levels should be universal and conducted without conditions attached. The international community should support the strengthening and promoting of democracy, development and respect for human rights and fundamental freedoms in the entire world.

9. The World Conference on Human Rights reaffirms that least developed countries committed to the process of democratisation and economic reforms, many of which are in Africa, should be supported by the international community in order to succeed in their transition to democracy and economic development.

10. The World Conference on Human Rights reaffirms the right to development, as established in the Declaration on the Right to Development, as a universal and inalienable right and an integral part of fundamental human rights.

As stated in the Declaration on the Right to Development, the human person is the central subject of development.

While development facilitates the enjoyment of all human rights, the lack of development may not be invoked to justify the abridgement of internationally recognised human rights.

States should cooperate with each other in ensuring development and eliminating obstacles to development. The international community should promote an effective international cooperation for the realisation of the right to development and the elimination of obstacles to development.

Lasting progress towards the implementation of the right to development requires effective development policies at the national level, as well as equitable economic relations and a favourable economic environment at the international level.

11. The right to development should be fulfilled so as to meet equitably the developmental and environmental needs of present and future generations. The World Conference on Human Rights recognises that illicit dumping of toxic and dangerous substances and waste potentially constitutes a serious threat to the human rights to life and health of everyone.

Consequently, the World Conference on Human Rights calls on all States to adopt and vigorously implement existing conventions relating to the dumping of toxic and dangerous products and waste and to cooperate in the prevention of illicit dumping.

Everyone has the right to enjoy the benefits of scientific progress and its applications. The World Conference on Human Rights notes that certain advances, notably in the biomedical and life sciences as well as in information technology, may have potentially adverse consequences for the integrity, dignity and human rights of the individual, and calls for international cooperation to ensure that human rights and dignity are fully respected in this area of universal concern.

12. The World Conference on Human Rights calls upon the international community to make all efforts to help alleviate the external debt burden of developing countries, in order to supplement the efforts of the Governments of such countries to attain the full realisation of the economic, social and cultural rights of their people.

13. There is a need for States and international organisations, in cooperation with non-governmental organisations, to create favourable conditions at the national, regional and international levels to ensure the full and effective enjoyment of human rights. States should eliminate all violations of human rights and their causes, as well as obstacles to the enjoyment of these rights.

14. The existence of widespread extreme poverty inhibits the full and effective enjoyment of human rights; its immediate alleviation and eventual elimination must remain a high priority for the international community.

15. Respect for human rights and for fundamental freedoms without distinction of any kind is a fundamental rule of international human rights law. The speedy and comprehensive elimination of all forms of racism and racial discrimination, xenophobia and related intolerance is a priority task for the international community. Governments should take effective measures to prevent and combat them. Groups, institutions intergovernmental and non-governmental organisations and individuals are urged to intensify their efforts in cooperating and coordinating their activities against these evils.

16. The World Conference on Human Rights welcomes the progress made in dismantling apartheid and calls upon the international community and the United Nations system to assist in this process.

The World Conference on Human Rights also deplores the continuing acts of violence aimed at undermining the quest for a peaceful dismantling of apartheid.

17. The acts, methods and practices of terrorism in all its forms and manifestations as well as linkage in some countries to drug trafficking are activities aimed at the destruction of human rights, fundamental freedoms and democracy, threatening territorial integrity, security of States and destabilizing legitimately constituted Governments. The international community should take the necessary steps to enhance cooperation to prevent and combat terrorism.

18. The human rights of women and of the girl-child are an inalienable, integral and indivisible part of universal human rights. The full and equal participation of women in political, civil, economic, social and cultural life, at the national, regional and international levels, and the eradication of all forms of discrimination on grounds of sex are priority objectives of the international community.

Gender-based violence and all forms of sexual harassment and exploitation, including those resulting from cultural prejudice and international trafficking, are incompatible with the dignity and worth of the human person, and must be eliminated. This can be achieved by legal measures and through national action and international cooperation in such fields as economic and social development, education, safe maternity and health care, and social support.

The human rights of women should form an integral part of the United Nations human rights activities, including the promotion of all human rights instruments relating to women.

The World Conference on Human Rights urges Governments, institutions intergovernmental and non-governmental organisations to intensify their efforts for the protection and promotion of human rights of women and the girl-child.

19. Considering the importance of the promotion and protection of the rights of persons belonging to minorities

and the contribution of such promotion and protection to the political and social stability of the States in which such persons live,

The World Conference on Human Rights reaffirms the obligation of States to ensure that persons belonging to minorities may exercise fully and effectively all human rights and fundamental freedoms without any discrimination and in full equality before the law in accordance with the declaration on the Rights of Persons Belonging to National or Ethnic, Religious and Linguistic Minorities.

The persons belonging to minorities have the right to enjoy their own culture, to profess and practise their own religion and to use their own language in private and in public, freely and without interference or any form of discrimination.

20. The World Conference on Human rights recognises the inherent dignity and the unique contribution of indigenous people to the development and plurality of society and strongly reaffirms the commitment of the international community to their economic, social and cultural well-being and their enjoyment of the fruits of sustainable development. States should ensure the full and free participation of indigenous people in all aspects of society, in particular in matters of concern to them. Considering the importance of the promotion and protection of the rights of indigenous people, and the contribution of such promotion and protection to the political and social stability of the States in which such people live, States should, in accordance with international law, take concerted positive steps to ensure respect for all human rights and fundamental freedoms of indigenous people, on the basis of equality and non-discrimination, and recognise the value and diversity of their distinct identities, cultures and social organisation.

21. The World Conference on Human Rights, welcoming the early ratification of the Convention on the Rights of the Child by a large number of States and noting the recognition of the human rights of children in the World

Declaration on the Survival, Protection and Development of Children and Plan of Action adopted by the World Summit for Children, urges universal rectification of the Convention by 1995 and its effective implementation by States parties through the adoption of all the necessary legislative, administrative and other measures and the allocation to the maximum extent of the available resources. In all actions concerning children, non-discrimination and the best interest of the child should be primary considerations and the views of the child given due weight. National and international mechanisms and programmes should be strengthened for the defence and protection of children, in particular, the girl-child, abandoned children, street children, economically and sexually exploited children, including through child pornography, child prostitution or sale of organs, children victims of diseases including acquired immunodeficiency syndrome, refugee and displaced children, children in detention, children in armed conflict, as well as children victims of famine and drought and other emergencies. International cooperation and solidarity should be promoted to support the implementation of the Convention and the rights of the child should be a priority in the United Nations system-wide action on human rights.

The World Conference on Human Rights also stresses that the child for the full and harmonious development of his or her personality should grow up in a family environment which accordingly merits broader protection.

22. Special attention needs to be paid to ensuring non-discrimination, and the equal enjoyment of all human rights and fundamental freedoms by disabled persons, including their active participation in all aspects of society.

23. The World Conference on Human Rights reaffirms that everyone, without distinction of any kind, is entitled to the right to seek and to enjoy in other countries asylum from persecution, as well as the right to return to one's own country. In this respect it stresses the importance of the Universal Declaration of Human Rights, the 1951

Convention relating to the Status of Refugees, its 1967 Protocol and regional instruments. It expresses its appreciation to States that continue to admit and host large numbers of refugees in their territories, and to the Office of the United Nations High Commissioner for Refugees for its dedication to its task. It also expresses its appreciation to the United Nations Relief and Works Agency for Palestine Refugees in the Near East.

The World Conference on Human Rights recognises that gross violations of human rights, including in armed conflicts, are among the multiple and complex factors leading to displacement of people.

The World Conference on Human Rights recognises that, in view of the complexities of the global refugee crisis and in accordance with the Charter of the United Nations, relevant international instruments and international solidarity and in the spirit of burden-sharing, a comprehensive approach by the international community is needed in coordination and cooperation with the countries concerned and relevant organisations, bearing in mind the mandate of the United Nations High Commissioner for Refugees. This should include the development of strategies to address the root causes and effects of movements of refugees and other displaced persons, the strengthening of emergency preparedness and response mechanisms, the provision of effective protection and assistance, bearing in mind the special needs of women and children, as well as the achievement of durable solutions, primarily through the preferred solution of dignified and safe voluntary repatriation, including solutions such as those adopted by the international refugee conferences. The World Conference on Human Rights underlines the responsibilities of States, particularly as they relate to the countries of origin.

In the light of the comprehensive approach, the World Conference on Human Rights emphasises the importance of giving special attention including through intergovernmental and humanitarian organisations and finding lasting solutions to questions related to internally displaced persons including their voluntary and safe return and rehabilitation.

In accordance with the Charter of the United Nations and the principles of humanitarian law, the World Conference on Human Rights further emphasises the importance of and the need for humanitarian assistance to victims of all natural and man-made disasters.

24. Great importance must be given to the promotion and protection of the human rights of persons belonging to groups which have been rendered vulnerable, including migrant workers, the elimination of all forms of discrimination against them, and the strengthening and more effective implementation of existing human rights instruments. States have an obligation to create and maintain adequate measures at the national level, in particular in the fields of education, health and social support, for the promotion and protection of the rights of persons in vulnerable sectors of their populations and to ensure the participation of those among them who are interested in finding a solution to their own problems.

25. The World Conference on Human Rights affirms that extreme poverty and social exclusion constitute a violation of human dignity and that urgent steps are necessary to achieve better knowledge of extreme poverty and its causes, including those related to the problem of development, in order to promote the human rights of the poorest, and to put an end to extreme poverty and social exclusion and to promote the enjoyment of the fruits of social progress. It is essential for States to foster participation by the poorest people in the decision-making process by the community in which they live, the promotion of human rights and efforts to combat extreme poverty.

26. The World Conference on Human Rights welcomes the progress made in the codification of human rights instruments, which is a dynamic and evolving process, and urges the universal ratification of human rights treaties. All States are encouraged to accede to these international instruments; all States are encouraged to avoid, as far as possible, the resort to reservations.

27. Every State should provide an effective framework of remedies to redress human rights grievances or violations. The administration of justice, including law enforcement and prosecutorial agencies and, especially, and independent judiciary and legal profession in full conformity with applicable standards contained in international human rights instruments, are essential to the full and non-discriminatory realisation of human rights and indispensable to the processes of democracy and sustainable development. In this context, institutions concerned with the administration of justice should be properly funded, and an increased level of both technical and financial assistance should be provided by the international community. It is incumbent upon the United Nations to make use of special programmes of advisory services on a priority basis for the achievement of a strong and independent administration of justice.

28. The World Conference on Human Rights expresses its dismay at massive violations of human rights especially in the form of genocide, "ethnic cleansing" and systematic rape of women in war situations, creating mass exodus of refugees and displaced persons. While strongly condemning such abhorrent practices it reiterates the call that perpetrators of such crimes be punished and such practices immediately stopped.

29. The World Conference on Human Rights expresses grave concern about continuing human rights violations in all parts of the world in disregard of standards as contained in international human rights instruments and international humanitarian law and about the lack of sufficient and effective remedies for the victims.

The World Conference on Human Rights is deeply concerned about violations of human rights during armed conflicts, affecting the civilian population, especially women, children, the elderly and the disabled. The Conference therefore calls upon States and all parties to armed conflicts strictly to observe international humanitarian law, as set forth in the

Geneva Conventions of 1949 and other rules and principles of international law, as well as minimum standards for protection of human rights, as laid down in international conventions.

The World Conference on Human Rights reaffirms the right of the victims to be assisted by humanitarian organisations, as set forth in the Geneva Conventions of 1949 and other relevant instruments of international humanitarian law, and calls for the safe and timely access for such assistance.

30. The World Conference on Human Rights also expresses its dismay and condemnation that gross and systematic violations and situations that constitute serious obstacles to the full enjoyment of all human rights continue to occur in different parts of the world. Such violations and obstacles include, as well as torture and cruel, inhuman and degrading treatment or punishment, summary and arbitrary executions, disappearances, arbitrary detentions, all forms of racism, racial discrimination and apartheid, foreign occupation and alien domination, xenophobia, poverty, hunger and other denials of economic, social and cultural rights, religious intolerance, terrorism, discrimination against women and lack of the rule of law.

31. The World Conference on Human Rights calls upon States to refrain from any unilateral measure not in accordance with international law and the Charter of the United Nations that creates obstacles to trade relations among States and impedes the full realisation of the human rights set forth in the Universal Declaration of Human Rights and international human rights instruments, in particular the rights of everyone to a standard of living adequate for their health and well-being, including food and medical care, housing and the necessary social services. The World Conference on Human Rights affirms that food should not be used as a tool for political pressure.

32. The World Conference on Human Rights reaffirms the importance of ensuring the universality, objectivity and non-selectivity of the consideration of human rights issues.

33. The World Conference on Human Rights reaffirms that States are duty-bound, as stipulated in the Universal Declaration of Human Rights and the International Covenant on Economic, Social and Cultural Rights and in other international human rights instruments to ensure that education is aimed at strengthening the respect of human rights and fundamental freedoms. The World Conference on Human Rights emphasises the importance of incorporating the subject of human rights education programmes and calls upon States to do so. Education should promote understanding, tolerance, peace and friendly relations between the nations and all racial or religious groups and encourage the development of United Nations activities in pursuance of these objectives. Therefore, education on human rights and the dissemination of proper information, both theoretical and practical, play an important role in the promotion and respect of human rights with regard to all individuals without distinction of any kind such as race, sex, language or religion, and this should be integrated in the education policies at the national as well as international levels. The World Conference on Human Rights notes that resource constraints and institutional inadequacies may impede the immediate realisation of these objectives.

34. Increased efforts should be made to assist countries which so request to create the conditions whereby each individual can enjoy universal human rights and fundamental freedoms. Governments and the United Nations system as well as other multilateral organisations are urged to increase considerably the resources allocated to programmes aiming at the establishment and strengthening of national legislation, national institutions and related infrastructures which uphold the rule of law and democracy, electoral assistance, human rights awareness through training, teaching and education, popular participation and civil society.

The programmes of advisory services and technical cooperation under the Centre for Human Rights should be strengthened as well as made more efficient and transparent and thus become a major contribution to improving respect for human rights. States are called upon to increase their contributions to these programmes, both through promoting a larger allocation from the United Nations regular budget and through voluntary contributions.

35. The full and effective implementation of United Nations activities to promote and protect human rights must reflect the high importance accorded to human rights by the Charter of the United Nations and the demands of the United Nations human rights activities, as mandated by Member States. To this end, United Nations Human Rights activities should be provided with increased resources.

36. The World Conference on Human Rights reaffirms the important and constructive role played by national institutions for the promotion and protection of human rights, in particular in their advisory capacity to the competent authorities, their role in remedying human rights violations, in the dissemination of human rights information, and education in human rights.

The World Conference on Human Rights encourages the establishment and strengthening of national institutions, having regard to the "Principles relating to the status of national institutions" and recognizing that it is the right of each State to choose the framework which is best suited to its particular needs at the national level.

37. Regional arrangements play a fundamental role in promoting and protecting human rights. They should reinforce universal human rights standards, as contained in international human rights instruments, and their protection. The World Conference on Human Rights endorses efforts under way to strengthen these arrangements and to increase their effectiveness, while at the same time stressing the importance of cooperation with the United Nations human rights activities.

The World Conference on Human Rights reiterates the need to consider the possibility of establishing regional and sub-regional arrangements for the promotion and protection of human rights where they do not already exist.

38. The World Conference on Human Rights recognises the important role of non-governmental organizations in the promotion of all human rights and in humanitarian activities at national, regional and international levels. The World Conference on Human Rights appreciates their contribution to increasing public awareness of human rights issues, to the conduct of education, training and research in this field, and to the promotion and protection of all human rights and fundamental freedoms. While recognizing that the primary responsibility for standard-setting lies with States, the Conference also appreciates the contribution of non-governmental organisations to this process. In this respect, the World Conference on Human Rights emphasises the importance of continued dialogue and cooperation between Governments and non-governmental organisations. Non-governmental organisations and their members genuinely involved in the field of human rights should enjoy the rights and freedoms recognised in the Universal Declaration of Human Rights, and the protection of the national law. These rights and freedoms may not be exercised contrary to the purposes and principles of the United Nations. Non-governmental organisations should be free to carry out their human rights activities, without interference, within the framework of national law and the Universal Declaration of Human Rights.

39. Underlining the importance of objective, responsible and impartial information about human rights and humanitarian issues, the World Conference on Human Rights encourages the increased involvement of the media, for whom freedom and protection should be guaranteed within the framework of national law.

II

A. Increased Coordination on Human Rights Within the United Nations System

1. The World Conference on Human Rights recommends increased coordination in support of human rights and fundamental freedoms within the United Nations system. To this end, the World Conference on Human Rights urges all United Nations organs, bodies and the specialised agencies whose activities deal with human rights to cooperate in order to strengthen, rationalise and streamline their activities, taking into account the need to avoid unnecessary duplication. The World Conference on Human Rights also recommends to the Secretary-General that high-level officials of relevant United Nations bodies and specialised agencies at their annual meeting, besides coordinating their activities, also assess the impact of their strategies and policies on the enjoyment of all human rights.

2. Furthermore, the World Conference on Human Rights calls on regional organizations and prominent international and regional finance and development institutions to assess also the impact of their policies and programmes on the enjoyment of human rights.

3. The World Conference on Human Rights recognises that relevant specialised agencies and bodies and institutions of the United Nations system as well as other relevant intergovernmental organisations whose activities deal with human rights play a vital role in the formulation, promotion and implementation of human rights standards, within their respective mandates, and should take into account the outcome of the World Conference on Human Rights within their fields of competence.

4. The World Conference on Human Rights strongly recommends that a concerted effort be made to encourage and facilitate the ratification of and accession or succession to international human rights treaties and

protocols adopted within the framework of the United Nations system with the aim of universal acceptance. The Secretary-General, in consultation with treaty bodies, should consider opening a dialogue with States not having acceded to these human rights treaties, in order to identify obstacles and to seek ways of overcoming them.

5. The World Conference on Human Rights encourages States to consider limiting the extent of any reservations they lodge to international human rights instruments, formulate any reservations as precisely and narrowly as possible, ensure that none is incompatible with the object and purpose of the relevant treaty and regularly review any reservations with a view to withdrawing them.

6. The World Conference on Human Rights, recognizing the need to maintain consistency with the high quality of existing international standards and to avoid proliferation of human rights instruments, reaffirms the guidelines relating to the elaboration of new international instruments contained in General Assembly resolution 41/120 of 4 December 1986 and calls on the United Nations human rights bodies, when considering the elaboration of new international standards, to keep those guidelines in mind to consult with human rights treaty bodies on the necessity for drafting new standards and to request the Secretariat to carry out technical reviews of proposed new instruments.

7. The World Conference on Human Rights recommends that human rights officers be assigned if and when necessary to regional offices of the United Nations Organisation with the purpose of disseminating information and offering training and other technical assistance in the field of human rights upon the request of concerned Member States. Human rights training for international civil servants who are assigned to work relating to human rights should be organised.

8. The World Conference on Human Rights welcomes the convening of emergency sessions of the Commission on

Human Rights as a positive initiative and that other ways of responding to acute violations of human rights be considered by the relevant organs of the United Nations system.

Resources

9. The World Conference on Human Rights, concerned by the growing disparity between the activities of the Centre for Human Rights and the Human, financial and other resources available to carry them out, and bearing in mind the resources needed for other important United Nations programmes, requests the Secretary-General and the General Assembly to take immediate steps to increase substantially the resources for the human rights programme from within the existing and future regular budgets of the United Nations, and to take urgent steps to seek increased extrabudgetary resources.

10. Within this framework, an increased proportion of the regular budget should be allocated directly to the Centre for Human Rights to cover its costs and all other costs borne by the Centre for Human Rights, including those related to the United Nations human rights bodies. Voluntary funding of the Centre's technical cooperation activities should reinforce this enhanced budget; the World Conference on Human Rights calls for generous contributions to the existing trust funds.

11. The World Conference on Human Rights requests the Secretary-General and the General Assembly to provide sufficient human, financial and other resources to the Centre for Human Rights to enable it effectively, efficiently and expeditiously to carry out its activities.

12. The World Conference on Human Rights, noting the need to ensure that human and financial resources are available to carry out the human rights activities, as mandated by inter-governmental bodies, urges the Secretary-General, in accordance with Article 101 of the Charter of the United Nations, and Member States to

adopt a coherent approach aimed at securing that resources commensurate to the increased mandates are allocated to the Secretariat. The World Conference on Human Rights invites the Secretary-General to consider whether adjustments to procedures in the programme budget cycle would be necessary or helpful to ensure the timely and effective implementation of human rights activities as mandated by Member States.

Centre for Human Rights

13. The World Conference on Human Rights stresses the importance of strengthening the United Nations Centre for Human Rights.

14. The Centre for Human Rights should play an important role in coordinating system-wide attention for human rights. The focal role of the Centre can best be realised if it is enabled to cooperate fully with other United Nations bodies and organs. The coordinating role of the Centre for Human Rights also implies that the office of the Centre for Human Rights in New York is strengthened.

15. The Centre for Human Rights should be assured adequate means for the system of thematic and country rapporteurs, experts, working groups and treaty bodies. Follow-up on recommendations should become a priority matter for consideration by the Commission on Human Rights.

16. The Centre for Human Rights should assume a larger role in the promotion of human rights. This role could be given shape through cooperation with Member States and by an enhanced programme of advisory services and technical assistance. The existing voluntary funds will have to be expanded substantially for these purposes and should be managed in a more efficient and coordinated way. All activities should follow strict and transparent project management rules and regular programme and project evaluations should be held periodically. To this

end, the results of such evaluation exercises and other relevant information should be made available regularly. The Centre should, in particular, organise at least once a year information meetings open to all Member States and organizations directly involved in these projects and programmes.

Adaptation and strengthening of the United Nations machinery for human rights, including the question of the establishment of a United Nations High Commissioner for Human Rights

17. The World Conference on Human Rights recognises the necessity for a continuing adaptation of the United Nations Human Rights machinery to the current and future needs in the promotion and protection of human rights, as reflected in the present Declaration and within the framework of a balanced and sustainable development for all people. In particular, the United Nations human rights organs should improve their coordination, efficiency and effectiveness.

18. The World Conference on Human Rights recommends to the General Assembly that, when examining the report of the Conference at its forty-eighth session, it begin, as a matter of priority, consideration of the question of the establishment of a High Commissioner for Human Rights for the promotion and protection of all human rights.

B. Equality, Dignity and Tolerance

1. Racism, racial discrimination, xenophobia and other forms of intolerance

19. The World Conference on Human Rights considers the elimination of racism and racial discrimination, in particular in their institutionalised forms such as apartheid or resulting from doctrines of racial superiority or exclusivity or contemporary forms and manifestations of racism, as a primary objective for the international community and a world-wide promotion programme in the field of human rights. United Nations organs and

agencies should strengthen their efforts to implement such a programme of action related to the third decade to combat racism and racial discrimination as well as subsequent mandates to the same end. The World Conference on Human Rights strongly appeals to the international community to contribute generously to the Trust Fund for the Programme for the Decade for Action to Combat Racism and Racial Discrimination.

20. The World Conference on Human Rights urges all Governments to take immediate measures and to develop strong policies to prevent and combat all forms and manifestations of racism, xenophobia or related intolerance, where necessary by enactment of appropriate legislation, including penal measures, and by the establishment of national institutions to combat such phenomena.

21. The World Conference on Human Rights welcomes the decision of the Commission on Human Rights to appoint a Special Rapporteur on contemporary forms of racism, racial discrimination, xenophobia and related intolerance. The World Conference on Human Rights also appeals to all States parties to the International Convention on the Elimination of All Forms of Racial Discrimination to consider making the declaration under article 14 of the Convention.

22. The World Conference on Human Rights calls upon all Governments to take all appropriate measures in compliance with their international obligations and with due regard to their respective legal systems to counter intolerance and related violence based on religion or belief, including practices of discrimination against women and including the desecration of religious sites, recognizing that every individual has the right to freedom of thought, conscience, expression and religion. The Conference also invites all States to put into practice the provisions of the Declaration on the Elimination of All Forms of Intolerance and of Discrimination Based on Religion or Belief.

23. The World Conference on Human Rights stresses that all persons who perpetrate or authorise criminal acts associated with ethnic cleansing are individually responsible and accountable for such human rights violations, and that the international community should exert every effort to bring those legally responsible for such violations to justice.

24. The World Conference on Human Rights calls on all States to take immediate measures, individually and collectively, to combat the practice of ethnic cleansing to bring it quickly to an end, Victims of the abhorrent practice of enthnic cleansing are entitled to appropriate and effective remedies.

2. Persons belonging to national or ethnic, religious and linguistic minorities

25. The World Conference on Human Rights calls on the Commission on Human Rights to examine ways and means to promote and protect effectively the rights of persons belonging to minorities as set out in the Declaration on the Rights of Persons belonging to National or Ethnic, Religious and Linguistic Minorities. In this context, the World Conference on Human Rights calls upon the Centre for Human Rights to provide, at the request of Governments concerned and as part of its programme of advisory services and technical assistance, qualified expertise on minority issues and human rights, as well as on the prevention and resolution of disputes, to assist in existing or potential situations involving minorities.

26. The World Conference on Human Rights urges States and the international community to promote and protect the rights of persons belonging to national or ethnic, religious and linguistic minorities in accordance with the Declaration on the Rights of Persons belonging to National or Ethnic, Religious and Linguistic Minorities.

27. Measures to be taken, where appropriate, should include facilitation of their full participation in all aspects of the

political, economic, social, religious and cultural life of society and in the economic progress and development in their country.

Indigenous People

28. The World Conference on Human Rights calls on the Working Group on Indigenous Populations of the Sub-commission on Prevention of Discrimination and Protection of Minorities to complete the drafting of a declaration on the rights of indigenous people at its eleventh session.

29. The World Conference on Human Rights recommends that the Commission on Human Rights consider the renewal and updating of the mandate of the Working Group on Indigenous Populations upon completion of the drafting of a declaration on the rights of indigenous people.

30. The World Conference on Human Rights also recommends that advisory services and technical assistance programmes within the United Nations system respond positively to requests by States for assistance which would be of direct benefit to indigenous people. The World Conference on Human Rights further recommends that adequate human and financial resources be made available to the Centre for Human Rights within the overall framework of strengthening the Centre's activities as envisaged by this document.

31. The World Conference on Human Rights urges States to ensure the full and free participation of indigenous people in all aspects of society, in particular in matters of concern to them.

32. The World Conference on Human Rights recommends that the General Assembly proclaim an international decade of the world's indigenous people, to begin from January 1994, including action-orientated programmes, to be decided upon in partnership with indigenous people. An appropriate voluntary trust fund should be set up for this purpose. In the framework of such a decade, the

establishment of a permanent forum for indigenous people in the United Nations system should be considered.

Migrant Workers

33. The World Conference on Human Rights urges all States to guarantee the protection of the human rights of all migrant workers and their families.

34. The World Conference on Human Rights considers that the creation of conditions to foster greater harmony and tolerance between migrant workers and the rest of the society of the State in which they reside is of particular importance.

35. The World Conference on Human Rights invites States to consider the possibility of signing and ratifying, at the earliest possible, time, the International Convention on the Rights of All Migrant Workers and Members of Their Families.

3. The equal status and human rights of women

36. The World Conference on Human Rights urges the full and equal enjoyment by women of all human rights and that this be priority for Governments and for the United Nations. The World Conference on Human Rights also underlines the importance of the integration and full participation of women as both agents and beneficiaries in the development process, and reiterates the objectives established on global action for women towards sustainable and equitable development set forth in the Rio Declaration on Environment and Development and chapter 24 of Agenda 21, adopted by the United Nations Conference on Environment and Development (Rio de Janeiro, Brazil, 3-14 June 1992).

37. The equal status of women and the human rights of women should be integrated into the mainstream of United Nations system-wide activity. These issues should be regularly and systematically addressed throughout relevant United Nations bodies and mechanisms. In

particular, steps should be taken to increase cooperation and promote further integration of objectives and goals between the Commission on the Status of Women, the Commission on Human Rights, the Committee for the Elimination of Discrimination against Women, the United Nations Development Fund for Women, the United Nations Development Programme and other United Nations agencies. In this context, cooperation and coordination should be strengthened between the Centre for Human Rights and the Division for the Advancement of Women.

38. In particular, the World Conference on Human Rights stresses the importance of working towards the elimination of violence against women in public and private life, the elimination of all forms of sexual harassment, exploitation and trafficking in women, the elimination of gender bias in the administration of justice and the eradication of any conflicts which may arise between the rights of women and urges States to combat violence against women in accordance with its provisions. Violations of the human rights of women in situations of armed conflict are violations of the fundamental principles of international human rights and humanitarian law. All violations of this kind, including in particular murder, systematic rape, sexual slavery, and forced pregnancy, require a particularly effective response.

39. The World Conference on Human Rights urges the eradication of all forms of discrimination against women, both hidden and overt. The United Nations should encourage the goal of universal ratification by all States of the Convention on the Elimination of All Forms of Discrimination against Women by the year 2000. Ways and means of addressing the particularly large number of reservations to the Convention should be encouraged. *Inter alia,* the Committee on the Elimination of Discrimination against Women should continue its review of reservations to the Convention. States are urged to withdraw reservations that are contrary to the object and

purpose of the Convention or which are otherwise incompatible with international treaty law.

40. Treaty monitoring bodies should disseminate necessary information to enable women to make more effective use of existing implementation procedures in their pursuits of full and equal enjoyment of human rights and non-discrimination. New procedures should also be adopted to strengthen implementation of the commitment to women's equality and the human rights of women. The Commission on the Status of Women and the Committee on the Elimination of Discrimination against women should quickly examine the possibility of introducing the right of petition through the preparation on an optional protocol to the Convention on the Elimination of All Forms of Discrimination against Women. The World Conference on Human Rights welcomes the decision of the Commission on Human Rights to consider the appointment of a special rapporteur on violence against women at its fiftieth session.

41. The World Conference on Human Rights recognises the importance of the enjoyment by women of the highest standard of physical and mental health throughout their life-span. In the context of the World Conference on Women and the Convention on the Elimination of All Forms of Discrimination against Women, as well as the Proclamation of Tehran of 1968, the World Conference on Human Rights reaffirms, on the basis of equality between women and men, a women's right to accessible and adequate health care and the widest range of family planning services, as well as equal access to education at all levels.

42. Treaty monitoring bodies should include the status of women and the human rights of women in their deliberations and findings, making use of gender-specific data. States should be encouraged to supply information on the situation of women *de jure* and de facto in their reports to treaty monitoring bodies. The World

Conference on Human Rights notes with satisfaction that the Commission on Human Rights adopted at its forty-ninth session resolution 1993/46 of 8 March 1993 stating that rapporteurs and working groups in the field of human rights should also be encouraged to do so. Steps should also be taken by the Division for the Advancement of Women in cooperation with other United Nations bodies, specifically the Centre for Human Rights, to ensure that the human rights activities of the United Nations regularly address violations of women's human rights, including gender-specific abuses. Training for United Nations human rights and humanitarian relief personnel to assist them to recognise and deal with human rights abuses particular to women and to carry out their work without gender bias should be encouraged.

43. The World Conference on Human Rights urges Governments and regional and international organisations to facilitate the access of women to decision-making posts and their greater participation in the decision-making process. It encourages further steps within the United Nations Secretariat to appoint and promote women staff members in accordance with the Charter of the United Nations, and encourages other principal and subsidiary organs of the United Nations to guarantee the participation of women under conditions of equality.

44. The World Conference on Human Rights welcomes the World Conference on Women to be held in Beijing in 1995 and urges that human rights of women should play an important role in its deliberations, in accordance with the priority themes of the World Conference on Women of equality, development and peace.

4. The rights of the child

45. The World Conference on Human Rights reiterates the principle of "First Call for Children" and, in this respect, underlines the importance of major national and international efforts, especially those of the United Nations Children's Fund, for promoting respect for the

rights of the child to survival, protection, development and participation.

46. Measures should be taken to achieve universal ratification of the Convention on the Rights of the Child by 1995 and the universal signing of the World Declaration on the Survival, Protection and Development of Children and Plan of Action adopted by the World Summit for Children, as well as their effective implementation. The World Conference on Human Rights urges States to withdraw reservations to the Convention on the Rights of the Child contrary to the object and purpose of the Convention or otherwise contrary to international treaty law.

47. The World Conference on Human Rights urges all nations to undertake measures to the maximum extent of their available resources, with the support of international cooperation, to achieve the goal in the World Summit Plan of Action. The Conference calls on States to integrate the Convention on the Rights of the Child into their national action plans. By means of these national action plans and through international efforts, particular priority should be placed on reducing infant and maternal mortality rates, reducing malnutrition and illiteracy rates and providing access to safe drinking-water and to basic education. When ever so called for, national plans of action should be devised to combat devastating emergencies resulting from natural disasters and armed conflicts and the equally grave problem of children in extreme poverty.

48. The World Conference on Human Rights urges all States, with the support of international cooperation, to address the acute problem of children under especially difficult circumstances. Exploitation and abuse of children should be actively combated, including by addressing their root causes. Effective measures are required against female infanticide, harmful child labour, sale of children and organs, child prostitution, child pornography, as well as other forms of sexual abuse.

49. The World conference on Human Rights supports all measures by the United Nations and its specialised agencies to ensure the effective protection and promotion of human rights of the girl child. The World Conference on Human Rights urges States to repeal existing laws and regulations and remove customs and practices which discriminate against and cause harm to the girl child.

50. The World Conference on Human Rights strongly supports the proposal that the Secretary-General initiate a study into means of improving the protection of children in armed conflicts. Humanitarian norms should be implemented and measures taken in order to protect and facilitate assistance to children in war zones. Measures should include protection for children against indiscriminate use of all weapons of war, especially anti-personnel mines. The need for after-care and rehabilitation of children traumatised by war must be addressed urgently. The Conference calls on the Committee on the Rights of the Child to study the question of raising the minimum age of recruitment into armed forces.

51. The World Conference on Human Rights recommends that matters relating to human rights and the situation of children be regularly reviewed and monitored by all relevant organs and mechanisms of the United Nations system and by the supervisory bodies of the specialised agencies in accordance with their mandates.

52. The World Conference on Human Rights recognises the important role played by non-governmental organisations in the effective implementation of all human rights instruments and, in particular, the Convention on the Rights of the Child.

53. The World Conference on Human Rights recommends that the Committee on the Rights of the Child, with the assistance of the Centre for Human Rights, be enabled expeditiously and effectively to meet its mandate, especially in view of the unprecedented extent of ratification and subsequent submission of country reports.

5. Freedom from torture

54. The World Conference on Human Rights welcomes the ratification by many Member States of the Convention against Torture and Other Cruel, Inhuman or Degrading Treatment or Punishment and encourages its speedy ratification by all other Member States.

55. The World Conference on Human Rights emphasises that one of the most atrocious violations against human dignity is the act of torture, the result of which destroys the dignity and impairs the capability of victims to continue their lives and their activities.

56. The World Conference on Human Rights reaffirms that under human rights law and international humanitarian law, freedom from torture is a right which must be protected under all circumstances, including in times of internal or international disturbance or armed conflicts.

57. The World Conference on Human Rights therefore urges all States to put an immediate end to the practice of torture and eradicate this evil forever through full implementations of the Universal Declaration of Human Rights as well as the relevant conventions and, where necessary, strengthening of existing mechanisms. The World Conference on Human Rights calls on all States to cooperate fully with the Special Rapporteur on the question of torture in the fulfilment of his mandate.

58. Special attention should be given to ensure universal respect for, and effective implementation of, the Principles of Medical Ethics relevant to the Role of Health Personnel, particularly Physicians, in the Protection of Prisoners and Detainees against Torture and other Cruel, Inhuman or Degrading Treatment or Punishment adopted by the General Assembly of the United Nations.

59. The World Conference on Human Rights stresses the importance of further concrete action within the framework of the United Nations with the view to providing assistance to victims of torture and ensuring

more effective remedies for their physical, psychological and social rehabilitation. Providing the necessary resources for this purpose should be given high priority, *inter alia,* by additional contributions to the United Nations Voluntary Fund for the Victims of Torture.

60. States should abrogate legislation leading to impunity for those responsible for grave violations of human rights such as torture and prosecute such violations, thereby providing a firm basis for the rule of law.

61. The World Conference on Human Rights reaffirms that efforts to eradicate torture should, first and foremost, be concentrated on prevention and, therefore, calls for the early adoption of an optional protocol to the Convention against Torture and Other Cruel, Inhuman and Degrading Treatment or Punishment, which is intended to establish a preventive system of regular visits to places of detention.

Enforced Disappearances

62. The World Conference on Human Rights, welcoming the adoption by the General Assembly of the Declaration on the Protection of All Persons from Enforced Disappearance, calls upon all States to take effective legislative, administrative, judicial or other measures to prevent, terminate and punish acts of enforced disappearances. The World Conference on Human Rights reaffirms that it is the duty of all States, under any circumstances to make investigations whenever there is reason to believe that an enforced disappearance has taken place on a territory under their jurisdiction and, if allegations are confirmed, to prosecute its perpetrators.

6. The rights of the disabled person

63. The World Conference on Human Rights reaffirms that all human rights and fundamental freedoms are universal and thus unreservedly include persons with disabilities. Every person is born equal and has the same rights to life and welfare, education and work, living independently

and active participation in all aspects of society. Any direct discrimination or other negative discriminatory treatment of a disabled person is therefore a violation of his or her rights. The World Conference on Human Rights calls on Governments, where necessary, to adopt or adjust legislation to assure access to these and other rights for disabled persons.

64. The place of disabled persons is everywhere. Persons with disabilities should be guaranteed equal opportunity through the elimination of all socially determined barriers, be they physical, financial, social or psychological, which exclude or restrict full participation in society.

65. Recalling the World Programme of Action concerning Disabled Persons, adopted by the General Assembly at its thirty-seventh session, the World Conference on Human Rights calls upon the General Assembly and the Economic and Social Council to adopt the draft standard rules on the equalisation of opportunities for persons with disabilities, at their meetings in 1993.

C. COOPERATION, DEVELOPMENT AND STRENGTHENING OF HUMAN RIGHTS

66. The World Conference on Human Rights recommends that priority be given to national and international action to promote democracy, development and human rights.

67. Special emphasis should be given to measures to assist in the strengthening and building of institutions relating to human rights, strengthening of a pluralistic civil society and the protection of groups which have been rendered vulnerable. In this context, assistance provided upon the request of Governments for the conduct of free and fair elections, including assistance in the human rights aspects of elections and public information about elections, is of particular importance. Equally important is the assistance to be given to the strengthening of the rule of law, the promotion of freedom of expression and the administration of justice, and to the real and effective

participation of the people in the decision-making processes.

68. The World Conference on Human Rights stresses the need for the implementation of strengthened advisory services and technical assistance activities by the Centre for Human Rights. The Centre should make available to States upon request assistance on specific human rights issues, including the preparation of reports under human rights treaties as well as for the implementation of coherent and comprehensive plans of action for the promotion and protection of human rights. Strengthening the institutions of human rights and democracy, the legal protection of human rights, training of officials and others, broad-based education and public information aimed at promoting respect for human rights should all be available as components of these programmes.

69. The World Conference on Human Rights strongly recommends that a comprehensive programme be established within the United Nations in order to help States in the task of building and strengthening adequate national structures which have a direct impact on the overall observance of human rights and the maintenance of the rule of law. Such a programme, to be coordinated by the Centre for Human Rights, should be able to provide, upon the request of the interested Government, technical and financial assistance to national projects in reforming penal and correctional establishments, education and training of lawyers, judges and security forces in human rights, and any other sphere of activity relevant to the good functioning of the rule of law. That programme should make available to States assistance for the implementation of plans of action for the promotion and protection of human rights.

70. The World Conference on Human Rights request the Secretary-General of the United Nations to submit proposals to the United Nations General Assembly, containing alternatives for the establishment, structure,

operational modalities and funding of the proposed programme.

71. The World Conference on Human Rights recommends that each State consider the desirability of drawing up a national action plan identifying steps whereby that State would improve the promotion and protection of human rights.

72. The World Conference on Human Rights reaffirms that the universal and inalienable right to development, as established in the Declaration on the Right to Development, must be implemented and realised. In this context, the World Conference on Human Rights welcomes the appointment by the Commission on Human Rights of a thematic working group on the right to development and urges that the Working Group, in a consultation and cooperation with other organs and agencies of the United Nations system, promptly formulate, for early consideration by the United Nations General Assembly, comprehensive and effective measures to eliminate obstacles to the implementation and realisation of the Declaration on the Right to Development and recommending ways and means towards the realisation of the right to development by all States.

73. The World Conference on Human Rights recommends that non-governmental and other grass-roots organizations active in development and/or human rights should be enabled to play a major role on the national and international levels in the debate, activities and implementation relating to the right to development and, in cooperation with Governments, in all relevant aspects of development cooperation.

74. The World Conference on Human Rights appeals to Governments, competent agencies and institutions to increase considerably the resources devoted to building well-functioning legal systems able to protect human rights, and to national institutions working in this area.

Actors in the field of development cooperation should bear in mind that mutually reinforcing inter-relationship between development, democracy and human rights. Cooperation should be based on dialogue and transparency. The World Conference on Human Rights also calls for the establishment of comprehensive programmes, including resource banks of information and personnel with expertise relating to the strengthening of the rule of law and of democratic institutions.

75. The World Conference on Human Rights encourages the Commission on Human Rights, in cooperation with the Committee on Economic, Social and Cultural Rights, to continue the examination of optional protocols to the International Covenant on Economic, Social and Cultural Rights.

76. The World Conference on Human Rights recommends that more resources be made available for the strengthening or the establishment of regional arrangements for the promotion and protection of human rights under the programmes of advisory services and technical assistance of the Centre for Human Rights. States are encouraged to request assistance for such purposes as regional and subregional workshops, seminars and information exchanges designed to strengthen regional arrangements for the promotion and protection of human rights in accord with universal human rights standards as contained in international human rights instruments.

77. The World Conference on Human Rights supports all measures by the United Nations and its relevant specialised agencies to ensure the effective promotion and protection of trade union rights, as stipulated in the International Covenant on Economic, Social and Cultural Rights and other relevant international instruments. It calls on all States to abide fully by their obligations in this regard contained in international instruments.

D. Human Rights Education

78. The World Conference on Human Rights considers human rights education, training and public information essential for the promotion and achievement of stable and harmonious relations among communities and for fostering mutual understanding, tolerance and peace.

79. States should strive to eradicate illiteracy and should direct education towards the full development of the human personality and to the strengthening of respect of human rights and fundamental freedoms. The World Conference on Human Rights calls on all States and institutions to include human rights, humanitarian law, democracy and rule of law as subjects in the curricula of all learning institutions in formal and non-formal settings.

80. Human rights education should include peace, democracy, development and social justice, as set forth in international and regional human rights instruments, in order to achieve common understanding and awareness with a view to strengthening universal commitment to human rights.

81. Taking into account the World Plan of Action on Education for Human Rights and Democracy, adopted in March 1993 by the International Congress on Eduction for Human Rights and Democracy of the United Nations Educational, Scientific and Cultural Organization, and other human rights instruments, the World Conference on Human Rights recommends that States develop specific programmes and strategies for ensuring the widest human rights education and the dissemination of public information, taking particular account of the human rights needs of women.

82 Governments, with the assistance of integovernmental organizations, national institutions and non-governmental organizations, should promote an increased awareness of human rights and mutual tolerance. The World Conference on Human Rights underlines the importance

of strengthening the World Public Information Campaign for Human Rights carried out by the United Nations. They should initiate and support education in human rights and undertake effective dissemination of public information in this field. The advisory services and technical assistance programmes of the United Nations system should be able to respond immediately to requests from States for educational and training activities in the field of human rights as well as for special education concerning standards as contained in international human rights instruments and in humanitarian law and their application to special groups such as military forces, law enforcement personnel, police and the health profession. The proclamation of a United Nations decade for human rights education in order to promote, encourage and focus these educational activities should be considered.

E. Implementation and Monitoring Methods

83. The World Conference on Human Rights urges Governments to incorporate standards as contained in international human rights instruments in domestic legislation and to strengthen national structures, institutions and organs of society which play a role in promoting and safeguarding human rights.

84. The World Conference on Human Rights recommends the strengthening of United Nations activities and programmes to meet requests for assistance by States which want to establish or strengthen their own national institution for the promotion and protection of human rights.

85. The World Conference on Human Rights also encourages the strengthening of cooperation between national institutions for the promotion and protection of human rights, particularly through exchanges of information and experience, as well as cooperation with regional organizations and the United Nations.

86. The World Conference on Human Rights strongly recommends in this regard that representatives of national

institutions for the promotion and protection of human rights convene periodic meetings under the auspices of the Centre for Human Rights to examine ways and means of improving their mechanisms and sharing experiences.

87. The World Conference on Human Rights recommends to the human rights treaty bodies, to the meetings of chairpersons of the treaty bodies and to the meetings of States parties that they continue to take steps aimed at coordinating the multiple reporting requirements and guidelines for preparing State reports under the respective human rights conventions and study the suggestion that the submission of one overall report on treaty obligations undertaken by each State would make these procedures more effective and increase their impact.

88. The World Conference on Human Rights recommends that the States parties to international human rights instruments, the General Assembly and the Economic and Social Council should consider studying the existing human rights treaty bodies and the various thematic mechanisms and procedures with a view to promoting greater efficiency and effectiveness through better coordination of the various bodies, mechanisms and procedures, taking into account the need to avoid unnecessary duplication and overlapping of their mandates and tasks.

89. The World Conference on Human Rights recommends continued work on the improvement of the functioning, including the monitoring tasks, of the treaty bodies, taking into account multiple proposals made in this respect, in particular those made by the treaty bodies themselves and by the meetings of the chair-persons of the treaty bodies. The comprehensive national approach taken by the Committee on the Rights of the Child should also be encouraged.

90. The World Conference on Human Rights recommends that States parties to human rights treaties consider accepting all the available optional communication procedures.

91. The World Conference on Human Rights views with concern the issue of impunity of perpetrators of human rights violations, and supports the efforts of the Commission on Human Rights and the Subcommission on Prevention of Discrimination and Protection of Minorities to examine all aspects of the issue.

92. The World Conference on Human Rights recommends that the Commission on Human Rights examine the possibility for better implementation of existing human rights instruments at the international and regional levels and encourages the International Law Commission to continue its work on an international criminal court.

93. The World Conference on Human Rights appeals to States which have not yet done so to accede to the Geneva Conventions of 12 August 1949 and the Protocols thereto, and to take all appropriate national measures, including legislative ones, for their full implementation.

94. The World Conference on Human Rights recommends the speedy completion and adoption of the draft declaration on the right and responsibility of individuals, groups and organs of society to promote and protect universally recognised human rights and fundamental freedoms.

95. The World Conference on Human Rights underlines the importance of preserving and strengthening the system of special procedures, rapporteurs, representatives, experts and working groups of the Commission on Human Rights and the Subcommission on the Prevention of Discrimination and Protection on Minorities, in order to enable them to carry out their mandates in all countries throughout the world, providing them with the necessary human and financial resources. The procedures and mechanisms should be enabled to harmonise and rationalise their work through periodic meetings. All States are asked to cooperate fully with these procedures and mechanisms.

96. The World Conference on Human Rights recommends that the United Nations assume a more active role in the promotion and protection of human rights in ensuring full respect for international humanitarian law in all situations of armed conflict, in accordance with the purposes and principles of the Charter of the United Nations.

97. The World Conference on Human Rights, recognizing the important role of human rights components in specific arrangements concerning some peace-keeping operations by the United Nations, recommends that the Secretary-General take into account the reporting, experience and capabilities of the Centre for Human Rights and human rights mechanisms, in conformity with the Charter of the United Nations.

98. The strengthen the enjoyment of economic, social and cultural rights, additional approaches should be examined, such as a system of indicators to measure progress in the realisation of the rights set forth in the International Covenant on Economic, Social and Cultural Rights. There must be a concerted effort to ensure recognition of economic, social and cultural rights at the national, regional and international levels.

F. Follow-up to the World Conference on Human Rights

99. The World Conference on Human Rights recommends that the General Assembly, the Commission on Human Rights and other organs and agencies of the United Nations system related to human rights consider ways and means for the full implementation, without delay, of the recommendations contained in the present Declaration, including the possibility of proclaiming a United Nations decade for human rights. The World Conference on Human Rights further recommends that the Commission on Human Rights annually review the progress towards this end.

100. The World Conference on Human Rights requests the Secretary-General of the United Nations to invite on the occasion of the fiftieth anniversary of the Universal Declaration of Human Rights all States, all organs and agencies of the United Nations system related to human rights, to report to him on the progress made in the implementation of the present Declaration and to submit a report to the General Assembly at its fifty-third session, through the Commission on Human Rights and the Economic and Social Council. Likewise, regional and, as appropriate, national human rights institutions, as well as non-governmental organizations, may present their views to the Secretary-General on the progress made in the implementation of the present Declaration. Special attention should be paid to assessing the progress towards the goal of universal ratification of international human rights treaties and protocols adopted within the framework of the United Nations system.

Annex I

THE INTERNATIONAL BILL OF HUMAN RIGHTS

Introduction

Five major United Nations legal instruments exist to define and to guarantee the protection of human rights: the Universal Declaration of Human Rights (1984), the International Covenant on Economic, Social and Cultural Rights (1966), the International Covenant on Civil and Political Rights (1966) and the two Operational Protocols to the latter Covenant. The Declaration is a manifesto with primarily moral authority. The Covenants are treaties binding on the States which ratify them. Together they constitute the document known as the International Bill of Human Rights.

Preparation of an International Bill of Rights was a fundamental preoccupation of the United Nations. The Charter of the United Nations, agreed to in San Francisco in 1945, in seven different articles declared United Nations support for human rights and set up a Human Rights Commission. In its first session in January 1946, the General Assembly called for the Commission to work towards "the formulation of an international bill of rights". When the Commission on Human Rights began its work in February 1947, this item was its first priority.

The members of the Commission were immediately divided over whether the Bill should take the form of a proclamation or a treaty. As a compromise, they decided that the Bill should have three parts: a declaration proclaiming general principles, a "covenant or covenants" embodying these principles in a form which would be binding on States which ratified them, and "measures of implementation" or provisions for review of the way in which States carried out their covenant obligations. In less than two years, the Commission sent to its superior bodies, the Economic and Social Council and the General Assembly, a completed draft of a Universal Declaration of Human Rights. On 10 December 1948, the General Assembly adopted the Universal Declaration of Human Rights by a vote of 48 in favour, eight abstentions and no dissensions.

The same day, the Assembly adopted a resolution urging that the Commission continue giving priority to drafting a treaty which would give legal force to the Declaration. In 1951, the Commission produced a draft covenant which it sent to its parent body, the Economic and Social Council. Seeing the difficulties in embodying in one covenant two different categories of rights, the Council urged the General Assembly to approve the drafting of two covenants. The Assembly agreed, and requested the Commission to proceed. The Commission complied and produced two draft covenants—one on economic, social and cultural rights, the other on civil and political rights, the latter with an optional protocol, and providing also for measures of review of implementation of the Covenant provisions. On 16 December 1966, the Assembly voted unanimously to adopt the three instruments and open them for signature. The instruments, after their ratification by 35 United Nations Member States, entered into force in 1976.

On 15 December 1989, by a vote of 59 in favour to 26 against, with 48 abstentions, the General Assembly adopted the Second Optional Protocol to the International Covenant on Civil and Political Rights, aiming at the abolition of the death penalty. This Second Optional Protocol came into force in July 1991.

* * *

The Universal Declaration of Human Rights is the basic international statement of the inalienable and inviolable rights of all members of the human family. It is intended to serve as "the common standard of achievement for all peoples and all nations" in the effort to secure universal and effective recognition and observance of the rights and freedoms it lists.

The two Covenants relating to human rights provide internal protection for specified rights and freedoms. Both Covenants recognise the right of peoples to self-determination. Both have provisions barring all forms of discrimination in the exercise of human rights. Both have the force of law for the countries which ratify them.

The first treaty, the Covenant on Economic, Social and Cultural Rights, recognises the right to work and to free choice of employment, to fair wages, to form and join unions, to social security and to adequate standards of living conditions for their people. States' reports on their progress in promotion of these rights are reviewed by a committee of experts appointed by the Economic and Social Council.

The Covenant on Civil and Political Rights recognises the right of every human person to life, liberty and security of person, to privacy, to freedom from cruel, inhuman or degrading treatment and from torture, to freedom from slavery, to immunity from arbitrary arrest, to a fair trial, to recognition as a person before the law, to immunity from retroactive sentences, to freedom of thought, conscience and religion, to freedom of opinion and expression, to liberty of movement, including the right to emigrate, to peaceful assembly and to freedom of association.

The Covenant on Civil and Political Rights sets up a Human Rights Committee to consider progress reports from States which have ratified the Covenant. The Committee may also hear complaints by such States that other States which have ratified the Covenant have failed in upholding the obligations under the Covenant.

Under the Optional Protocol to the Civil and Political Covenant, individuals under certain circumstances may file complaints of human rights violations by ratifying States.

Under the Second Optional Protocol to the Civil and Political Covenant, States must take all necessary measures to abolish the death penalty.

The Declaration is accepted almost universally as a gauge by which Governments can measure their progress in the protection of human rights. In United Nations organs, the Declaration has an authority surpassed only by the Charter, It is invoked constantly not only in the General Assembly, but also in the Security Council and other organs. It is quoted in international legal instruments, including the Council of Europe's Convention for the Protection of Human Rights and Fundamental Freedoms (1950), the Japanese Peace Treaty (1951), the Special Statute for the status of Trieste (1954), the Constitution of the Organisation of African Unity (1963) and the Final Document of the Conference on Security and Cooperation in Europe (1975), signed at Helsinki by 35 States. It is invoked in a score of national constitutions. It has inspired and sometimes become part of many countries' national legislation, and has been cited with approval in national courts.

UNIVERSAL DECLARATION OF HUMAN RIGHTS

Preamble

Whereas recognition of the inherent dignity and of the equal and inalienable rights of all members of the human family is the foundation of freedom, justice and peace in the world,

Whereas disregard and contempt for human rights have resulted in barbarous acts which have outraged the conscience of mankind, and the advent of a world in which human beings shall enjoy freedom of speech and belief and freedom from fear and want has been proclaimed as the highest aspiration of the common people,

Whereas it is essential, if man is not to be compelled to have recourse, as a last resort, to rebellion against tyranny and oppression, that human rights should be protected by the rule of law,

Whereas it is essential to promote the development of friendly relations between nations,

Whereas the peoples of the United Nations have in the Charter reaffirmed their faith in fundamental human rights, in the dignity and worth of the human person and in the equal rights of men and women and have determined to promote social progress and better standards of life in larger freedom.

Whereas Member States have pledged themselves to achieve, in co-operation with the United Nations, the promotion of universal respect for and observance of human rights and fundamental freedoms,

Whereas a common understanding of these rights and freedoms is the greatest importance for the full realisation of this pledge,

Now, therefore, The General Assembly *proclaims*

This Universal Declaration of human Rights as a common standard of achievement for all peoples and all nations, to the end that every individual and every organ of society, keeping this Declaration constantly in mind, shall strive by teaching and education to promote respect for these rights and freedoms and by progressive measures, national and international, to secure their universal and effective recognition and observance, both among the peoples of Member States themselves and among the peoples of territories under their jurisdiction.

Article 1

All human beings are born free and equal in dignity and rights. They are endowed with reason and conscience and should act towards one another in a spirit of brotherhood.

Article 2

Everyone is entitled to all the rights and freedoms set forth in this Declaration, without distinction of any kind, such as race, colour, sex, language, religion, political or other opinion, national or social origin, property, birth or other status.

Furthermore, non distinction shall be made on the basis of the political, jurisdictional or international status of the country or territory to which a person belongs, whether it be independent, trust, non-self-governing or under any other limitation of sovereignty.

Article 3

Everyone has the right to life, liberty and security of person.

Article 4

No one shall be held in slavery or servitude; slavery and the slave trade shall be prohibited in all their forms.

Article 5

No one shall be subjected to torture or to cruel, inhuman or degrading treatment or punishment.

Article 6

Everyone has the right to recognition everywhere as a person before the law.

Article 7

All are equal before the law and are entitled without any discrimination to equal protection of the law. All are entitled to equal protection against any discrimination in violation of this Declaration and against any incitement to such discrimination.

Article 8

Everyone has the right to an effective remedy by the competent national tribunals for acts violating the fundamental rights granted him by the constitution or by law.

Article 9

No one shall be subjected to arbitrary arrest, detention or exile.

Article 10

Everyone is entitled in full equality to a fair and public hearing by an independent and impartial tribunal, in the determination of his rights and obligations and of any criminal charge against him.

Article 11

1. Everyone charged with a penal offence has the right to be presumed innocent until proved guilty according to

law in a public trial at which he has had all the guarantees necessary for his defence.

2. No one shall be held guilty of any penal offence on account of any act or omission which did not constitute a penal offence, under national or international law, at the time when it was committed. Nor shall a heavier penalty be imposed than the one that was applicable at the time the penal offence was committed.

Article 12

No one shall be subjected to arbitrary interference with his privacy, family, home or correspondence, nor to attacks upon his honour and reputation. Everyone has the right to the protection of the law against such interference or attacks.

Article 13

1. Everyone has the right to freedom of movement and residence within the borders of each state.

2. Everyone has the right to leave any country, including his own, and to return to his country.

Article 14

1. Everyone has the right to seek and to enjoy in other countries asylum from persecution.
2. This right may not be invoked in the case of prosecutions genuinely arising from non-political crimes or from acts contrary to the purposes and principles of the United Nations.

Article 15

1. Everyone has the right to a nationality.
2. No one shall be arbitrarily deprived of his nationality, nor denied the right to change his nationality.

Article 16

1. Men and women of full age, without any limitation due to race, nationality or religion, have the right to marry and to found a family.

They are entitled to equal rights as to marriage, during marriage and at its dissolution.

2. Marriage shall be entered into only with the free and full consent of the intending spouses.

3. The family is the natural and fundamental group unit of society and is entitled to protection by society and the State.

Article 17

1. Everyone has the right to own property alone as well as in association with others.

2. No one shall be arbitrarily deprived of his property.

Article 18

Everyone has the right to freedom of thought, conscience and religion; this right includes freedom to change his religion or belief, and freedom, either alone or in community with others and in public or private to manifest his religion or belief in teaching, practice, worship and observance.

Article 19

Everyone has the right to freedom of opinion and expression; this right includes freedom to hold opinions without interference and to seek, receive and impart information and ideas through any media and regardless of frontiers.

Article 20

1. Everyone has the right to freedom of peaceful assembly and association.

2. No one may be compelled to belong to an association.

Article 21

1. Everyone has the right to take part in the government of his country, directly or through freely chosen representatives.

2. Everyone has the right of equal access to public service in his country.

3. The will of the people shall be the basis of the authority of government; this will shall be expressed in periodic

and genuine elections which shall be by universal and equal suffrage and shall be held by secret vote or by equivalent free voting procedures.

Article 22

Everyone, as a member of society, has the right to social security and is entitled to realization, through national effort and international cooperation and in accordance with the organisation and resources of each State, of the economic, social and cultural rights indispensable for his dignity and the free development of his personality.

Article 23

1. Everyone has the right to work, to free choice of employment, to just and favourable conditions of work and to protection against unemployment.
2. Everyone, without any discrimination, has the right to equal pay for equal work.
3. Everyone who works has the right to just and favourable remuneration ensuring for himself and his family an existence worthy of human dignity, and supplemented, if necessary, by other means of social protection.
4. Everyone has the right to form and to join trade unions for the protection of his interests.

Article 24

Everyone has the right to rest and leisure, including reasonable limitation of working hours and periodic holidays with pay.

Article 25

1. Everyone has the right to a standard of living adequate for the health and well-being of himself and of his family, including food, clothing housing and medical care and necessary social services, and the right to security in the event of unemployment, sickness, disability, widowhood, old age or other lack of livelihood in circumstances beyond his control.

2. Motherhood and childhood are entitled to special care and assistance. All children, whether born in or out of wedlock, shall enjoy the same social protection.

Article 26

1. Everyone has the right to education. Education shall be free, at least in the elementary and fundamental stages. Elementary education shall be compulsory. Technical and professional education shall be made generally available and higher education shall be equally accessible to all on the basis of merit.

2. Educational shall be directed to the full development of the human personality and to the strengthening of respect for human rights and fundamental freedoms. It shall promote understanding, tolerance and friendship among all nations, racial or religious groups. And shall further the activities of the United Nations for the maintenance of peace.

3. Parents have a prior right to choose the kind of education that shall be given to their children.

Article 27

1. Everyone has the right freely to participate in the cultural life of the community, to enjoy the arts and to share in scientific advancement and its benefits.

2. Everyone has the right to the protection of the moral and material interests resulting from any scientific, literary or artistic production of which he is the author.

Article 28

Everyone is entitled to a social and international order in which the rights and freedoms set forth in this Declaration can be fully realised.

Article 29

1. Everyone has duties to the community in which alone the free and full development of his personality is possible.

2. In the exercise of his rights and freedoms, everyone shall be subject only to such limitations as are determined by

law solely for the purpose of securing due recognition and respect for the rights and freedoms of others and of meeting the just requirements of morality, public order and the general welfare in a democratic society.

3. These rights and freedoms may in no case be exercised contrary to the purposes and principles of the United Nations.

Article 30

Nothing in this Declaration may be interpreted as implying for any State, group or person any right to engage in any activity or to perform any act aimed at the destruction of any of the rights and freedoms set fourth herein.

INTERNATIONAL COVENANT ON ECONOMIC, SOCIAL AND CULTURAL RIGHTS

Preamble

The States Parties to the Present Covenant,

Considering that, in accordance with the principles proclaimed in the Charter of the United Nations, recognition of the inherent dignity and of the equal and inalienable rights of all members of the human family is the foundation of freedom, justice and peace in the world,

Recognizing that these rights derive from the inherent dignity of the human person,

Recognizing that, in accordance with the Universal Declaration of Human Rights, the ideal of free human beings enjoying freedom from fear and want can only be achieved if conditions are created whereby everyone may enjoy his economic, social and cultural rights, as well as his civil and political rights,

Considering the obligation of States under the Charter of the United Nations to promote universal respect for, and observance of, human rights and freedoms,

Realizing that the individual, having duties to other individuals and to the community to which he belongs, is under a responsibility to strive for the promotion and observance of the rights recognised in the present Covenant,

Agree upon the following articles:

Part 1

Article 1

1. All peoples have the right of self-determination. By virtue of that right they freely determine their political status and freely pursue their economic, social and cultural development.

2. All peoples may, for their own ends, freely dispose of their natural wealth and resources without prejudice to any obligations arising out of international economic co-operation, based upon the principle of mutual benefit, and international law. In no case may a people be deprived of its own means of subsistence.

3. The States Parties to the present Covenant, including those having responsibility for the administration of Non-Self-Governing and Trust Territories, shall promote the realisation of the right of self-determination, and shall respect that right, in conformity with the provisions of the Charter of the United Nations.

Part II

Article 2

1. Each State Party to the present Covenant undertakes to take steps, individually and through international assistance and co-operation, especially economic and technical, to the maximum of its available resources, with a view to achieving progressively the full realisation of the rights recognised in the present Covenant by all appropriate means, including particularly the adoption of legislative measures.

2. The States Parties to the present Covenant undertake to guarantee that the rights enunciated in the present

Covenant will be exercised without discrimination of any kind as to race, colour, sex, language, religion, political or other opinion, national or social origin, property, birth or other status.

3. Developing countries, with due regard to human rights and their national economy, may determine to what extent they would guarantee the economic rights recognised in the present Covenant to non-nationals.

Article 3

The States Parties to the present Covenant undertake to ensure the equal right of men and women to the enjoyment of all economic, social and cultural rights set forth in the present Covenant.

Article 4

The States Parties to the present Covenant recognise that, in the enjoyment of those rights provided by the State in conformity with the present Covenant, the State may subject such rights only to such limitations as are determined by law only in so far as this may be compatible with the nature of these rights and solely for the purpose of promoting the general welfare in a democratic society.

Article 5

1. Nothing in the present Covenant may be interpreted as implying for any State, group or person any right to engage in any activity or to perform any act aimed at the destruction of any of the rights or freedoms recognised herein, or at their limitation to a greater extent than is provided for in the present Covenant.

2. No restriction upon or derogation from any of the fundamental human rights recognised or existing in any country in virtue of law, conventions, regulations or custom shall be admitted on the pretext that the present Covenant does not recognise such rights or that it recognises them to a lesser extent.

Part III

Article 6

1. The States Parties to the present Covenant recognise the right to work, which includes the right of everyone to the opportunity to gain his living by work which he freely chooses or accepts, and will take appropriate steps to safeguard this right.

2. The steps to be taken by a State Party to the present Covenant to achieve the full realisation of this right shall include technical and vocational guidance and training programmes, policies and techniques to achieve steady economic, social and cultural development and full and productive employment under conditions safeguarding fundamental political and economic freedoms to the individual.

Article 7

The States Parties to the present Covenant recognise the right of everyone to the enjoyment of just and favourable conditions of work which ensure, in particular:

(a) Remuneration which provides will workers, as a minimum, with:

(i) Fair wages and equal remuneration for work of equal value without distinction of any kind, in particular women being guaranteed conditions of work not inferior to those enjoyed by men, with equal pay for equal work;

(ii) A decent living for themselves and their families in accordance with the provisions of the present Covenant;

(b) Safe and healthy working conditions;

(c) Equal opportunity for everyone to the promoted in his employment to an appropriate higher level, subject to no considerations other than those of seniority and competence;

(d) Rest, leisure and reasonable limitation of working hours and periodic holidays with pay, as well as remuneration for public holidays.

Article 8

1. The States Parties to the present Covenant undertake to ensure:

   (a) The right of everyone to form trade unions and join the trade union of his choice, subject only to the rules of the organisation concerned, for the promotion and protection of this economic and social interests. No restrictions may be placed on the exercise of this right other than those prescribed by law and which are necessary in a democratic society in the interests of national security or public order or for the protection of the rights and freedoms of others;

   (b) The right of trade unions to establish national federations or confederations and the right of the latter to form or join international trade-union organizations;

   (c) The right of trade unions to function freely subject to no limitations other than those prescribed by law and which are necessary in a democratic society in the interests of national security or public order or for the protection of the rights and freedoms of others;

   (d) The right to strike, provided that it is exercised in conformity with the laws of the particular country.

2. This article shall not prevent the imposition of lawful restrictions on the exercise of these rights by members of the armed forces or of the police or of the administration of the State.

3. Nothing in this article shall authorise States Parties to the International Labour Organisation Convention of 1948 concerning Freedom of Association and Protection of the

Right to Organise to take legislative measures which would prejudice, or apply the law in such a manner as would prejudice, the guarantees provided for in that Convention.

Article 9

The States Parties to the present Covenant recognise the right of everyone to social security, including social insurance.

Article 10

The States Parties to the present Covenant recognise that:

1. The widest possible protection and assistance should be accorded to the family, which is the natural and fundamental group unit of society, particularly for its establishment and while it is responsible for the care and education of dependent children. Marriage must be entered into with the free consent of the intending spouses.

2. Special protection should be accorded to mothers during a reasonable period before and after childbirth. During such period working mothers should be accorded paid leave or leave with adequate social security benefits.

3. Special measures of protection and assistance should be taken on behalf of all children and young persons without any discrimination for reasons of parentage or other conditions. Children and young persons should be protected from economic and social exploitation. Their employment in work harmful to their morals or health or dangerous to life or likely to hamper their normal development should be punishable by law. States should also set age limits below which the paid employment of child labour should be prohibited and punishable by law.

Article 11

1. The States Parties to the present Covenant recognise the right of everyone to an adequate standard of living

for himself and his family, including adequate food, clothing and housing, and to the continuous improvement of living conditions. The States Parties will take appropriate steps to ensure the realisation of this right, recognizing to this effect the essential importance of international co-operation based on free consent.

2. The States Parties to the present Covenant, recognizing the fundamental right of everyone to be free from hunger, shall take, individually and through international cooperation, the measures, including specific programmes, which are needed:

   (a) To improve methods of production, conservation and distribution of food by making full use of technical and scientific knowledge, by disseminating knowledge of the principles of nutrition and by developing or reforming agrarian systems in such a way as to achieve the most efficient development and utilisation of natural resources:

   (b) Taking into account the problems of both food-importing and food-exporting countries, to ensure an equitable distribution of world food supplies in relation to need.

Article 12

1. The States parties to the present Covenant recognise the right of everyone to the enjoyment of the highest attainable standard of physical and mental health.

2. The steps to be taken by the States Parties to the present Covenant to achieve the full realisation of this right shall include those necessary for:

   (a) The provision for the reduction of the stillbirth-rate and of infant mortality and for the healthy development of the child;

   (b) The improvement of all aspects of environmental and industrial hygiene;

   (c) The prevention, treatment and control of epidemic, endemic, occupational and other diseases;

(d) The creation of conditions which would assure to all medical service and medical attention in the event of sickness.

Article 13

1. The States Parties to the present Covenant recognise the right of everyone to education. They agree that education shall be directed to the full development of the human personality and the sense of its dignity, and shall strengthen the respect for human rights and fundamental freedoms. They further agree that education shall enable all persons to participate effectively in a free society, promote understanding, tolerance and friendship among all nations and all racial, ethnic or religious groups, and further the activities of the United Nations for the maintenance of peace.

2. The States Parties to the present Covenant recognise that, with a view to achieving the full realisation of this right:

   (a) Primary education shall be compulsory and available free to all;

   (b) Secondary education in its different forms, including technical and vocational secondary education, shall be made generally available and accessible to all by every appropriate means, and in particular by the progressive introduction of free education;

   (c) Higher education shall be made equally accessible to all, on the basis of capacity, by every appropriate means, and in particular by the progressive introduction of free education;

   (d) Fundamental education shall be encouraged or intensified as far as possible for those persons who have not received or completed the whole period of their primary education;

   (e) The development of a system of schools at all levels shall be actively pursued, an adequate fellowship system shall be established, and the material conditions of teaching staff shall be continuously improved.

3. The States Parties to the present Covenant undertake to have respect for the liberty of parents and, when applicable, legal guardians to choose for their children schools, other than those established by the public authorities, which conform to such minimum educational standards as may be laid down or approved by the State and to ensure the religious and moral education of their children in conformity with their own convictions.

4. No part of this article shall be construed so as to interfere with the liberty of individuals and bodies to establish and direct educational institutions, subject always to the observance of the principles set fourth in paragraph 1 of this article and to the requirement that the education given in such institutions shall conform to such minimum standards as may be laid down by the State.

Article 14

Each State Party to the present Covenant which, at the time of becoming a Party, has not been able to secure in its metropolitan territory or other territories under its jurisdiction compulsory primary education, free of charge, undertakes, within two years, to work out and adopt a detailed plan of action for the progressive implementation, within a reasonable number of years, to be fixed in the plan, of the principle of compulsory education free of charge for all.

Article 15

1. The States Parties to the present Covenant recognise the right of everyone:

   (a) To take part in cultural life;

   (b) To enjoy the benefits of scientific progress and its applications;

   (c) To benefit from the protection of the moral and material interests resulting from any scientific, literary or artistic production of which he is the author.

2. The steps to be taken by the States Parties to the present Covenant to achieve the full realisation of this right shall include those necessary for the conservation, the development and the diffusion of science and culture.

3. The States Parties to the present Covenant undertake to respect the freedom indispensable for scientific research and creative activity.

4. The States Parties to the present Covenant recognise the benefits to be derived from the encouragement and development of international contacts and co-operation in the scientific and cultural fields.

Part IV

Article 16

1. The States parties to the present Covenant undertake to submit in conformity with this part of the Covenant reports on the measures which they have adopted and the progress made in achieving the observance of the rights recognised herein.

2. **(a)** All reports shall be submitted to the Secretary-General of the United Nations, who shall transmit copies to the Economic and Social Council for consideration in accordance with the provisions of the present Covenant.

   (b) The secretary-General of the United Nations shall also transmit to the specialised agencies copies of the reports, or any relevant parts therefrom, from States Parties to the present Covenant which are also members of these specialised agencies in so far as these reports, or parts therefrom, relate to any matters which fall within the responsibilities of the said agencies in accordance with their constitutional instruments.

Article 17

1. The States Parties to the present Covenant shall furnish their reports in stages, in accordance with a programme to be established by the Economic and Social Council within one year of the entry into force of the present Covenant after consultation with the States Parties and the specialised agencies concerned.
2. Reports may indicate factors and difficulties affecting the degree of fulfilment of obligations under the present Covenant
3. Where relevant information has previously been furnished to the United Nations or to any specialised agency by any State Party to the present Covenant, it will not be necessary to reproduce that information, but a precise reference to the information so furnished will suffice.

Article 18

Pursuant to its responsibilities under the Charter of the United Nations in the field of human rights and fundamental freedoms, the Economic and Social Council may make arrangements with the specialised agencies in respect of their reporting to it on the progress made in achieving the observance of the provisions of the present Covenant falling within the scope of their activities. These reports may include particulars of decisions and recommendations on such implementation adopted by their competent organs.

Article 19

The Economic and Social Council may transmit to the Commission on Human Rights for study and general recommendations or, as appropriate, for information the reports concerning human rights submitted by States in Accordance with articles 16 and 17, and those concerning human rights submitted by the specialised agencies in accordance with article 18.

Article 20

The States Parties to the present Covenant and the specialised agencies concerned may submit comments to the

Economic and Social Council on any general recommendation under article 19 or reference to such general recommendation in any report of the Commission on Human Rights or any documentation referred to therein.

Article 21

The Economic and Social Council may submit from time to time to the General Assembly reports with recommendations of a general nature and a summary of the information received from the States Parties to the present Covenant and the specialised agencies on the measures taken and the progress made in achieving general observance of the rights recognised in the present Covenant.

Article 22

The Economic and Social Council may bring to the attention of other organs of the United Nations, their subsidiary organs and specialised agencies concerned with furnishing technical assistance any matters arising out of the reports referred to in this part of the present Covenant which may assist such bodies in deciding, each within its field of competence, on the advisability of international measures likely to contribute to the effective progressive implementation of the present Covenant.

Article 23

The States Parties to the present convenant agree that international action for the achievement of the rights recognised in the present Covenant includes such methods as the conclusion of conventions, the adoption of recommendations, the furnishing of technical assistance and the holding of regional meetings and technical meetings for the purpose of consultation and study organised in conjunction with the Governments concerned.

Article 24

Nothing in the present Covenant shall be interpreted as impairing the provisions of the Charter of the United Nations and of the constitutions of the specialised agencies which define the respective responsibilities of the various organs of the

United Nations and of the specialised agencies in regard to the matters dealt with in the present Covenant.

Article 25

Nothing in the present Covenant shall be interpreted as impairing the inherent right of all peoples to enjoy and utilise fully and freely their natural wealth and resources.

Part V

Article 26

1. The present Covenant is open for signature by any State Member of the United Nations or member of any of its specialised agencies, by any State Party to the Statue of the International Court of Justice, and by any other State which has been invited by the General Assembly of the United Nations to become a party to the present Covenant.
2. The present Covenant is subject to ratification. Instruments of ratification shall be deposited with the Secretary-General of the United Nations.
3. The present Covenant shall be open to accession by any State referred to in paragraph 1 of this article.
4. Accession shall be effected by the deposit of an instrument of accession with the Secretary-General of the United Nations.
5. The Secretary-General of the United Nations shall inform all States which have signed the present Covenant or acceded to it of the deposit of each instrument of ratification or accession.

Article 27

1. The present Covenant shall enter into force there months after the date of the deposit with the Secretary-General of the United Nations of the thirty-fifth instrument of ratification or instrument of accession.
2. For each State ratifying the present Covenant or acceding to it after the deposit of the thirty-fifth instrument of

ratification or instrument of accession, the present Covenant shall enter into force three months after the date of the deposit of its own instrument of ratification or instrument of accession.

Article 28

The provision of the present Covenant shall extend to all parts of federal States without any limitations or exceptions.

Article 29

1. Any State Party to the present Covenant may propose an amendment and file it with the Secretary-General of the United Nations. The Secretary-General shall thereupon communicate any proposed amendments to the States Parties to the present Covenant with a request that they notify him whether they favour a conference of States Parties for the purpose of considering and voting upon the proposals. In the event that at least one third of the States Parties favours such a conference, the Secretary-General shall convene the conference under the auspices of the United Nations. Any amendment adopted by a majority of the States Parties present and voting at the conference shall be submitted to the General Assembly of the United Nations for approval.

2. Amendments shall come into force when they have been approved by the General Assembly of the United Nations and accepted by a two-thirds majority of the States Parties to the present Covenant in accordance with their respective constitutional processes.

3. When amendments come into force they shall be binding on those States Parties which have accepted them, other States Parties still being bound by the provisions of the present Covenant and any earlier amendment which they have accepted.

Article 30

Irrespective of the notifications made under article 26, paragraph 5, the Secretary-General of the United Nations shall inform all States referred to in paragraph 1 of the same article of the following particulars:

(a) Signatures, ratifications and accessions under article 26;

(b) The date of the entry into force of the present Covenant under article 27 and the date of the entry into force of any amendments under article 29.

Article 31

1. The present Covenant, of which the Chinese, English, French, Russian and Spanish texts are equally authentic, shall be deposited in the archives of the United Nations.

2. The Secretary-General of the United Nations shall transmit certified copies of the present Covenant to all States referred to in article 26.

INTERNATIONAL COVENANT ON CIVIL AND POLITICAL RIGHTS

Preamble

The States Parties to the Present Covenant,

Considering that, in accordance with the principles proclaimed in the Charter of the United Nations, recognition of the inherent dignity and of the equal and inalienable rights of all members of the human family is the foundation of freedom, justice and peace in the world,

Recognizing that these right derive from the inherent dignity of the human person,

Recognizing that, in accordance with the Universal Declaration of Human Rights, the ideal of free human beings enjoying civil and political freedom end freedom from fear and want can only be achieved if conditions are created whereby everyone may enjoy his civil and political rights, as well as his economic social and cultural rights,

Considering the obligation of States under the Charter of the United Nations to promote universal respect for, and observance of, human rights and freedoms,

Realizing that the individual, having duties to other individuals and to the community to which he belongs, is under a responsibility to strive for the promotion and observance of the rights recognised in the present Covenant,

Agree upon the following articles:

Part 1

Article 1

1. All peoples have the right of self-determination. By virtue of that right they freely determine their political status and freely pursue their economic, social and cultural development.

2. All peoples may, for their own ends, freely dispose of their natural wealth and resources without prejudice to any obligations arising out of international economic co-operation, based upon the principle of mutual benefit, and international law. In no case may a people be deprived of its own means of subsistence.

3. The States Parties to the present Covenant, including those having responsibility for the administration of Non-Self-Governing and Trust Territories, shall promote the realisation of the right of self-determination, and shall respect that right, in conformity with the provision of the Charter of the United Nations.

Part II

Article 2

1. Each State Party to the present Covenant undertakes to respect and to ensure to all individuals within its territory and subject to its jurisdiction the rights recognised in the present Covenant, without distinction of any kind, such as race, colour, sex, language, religion, political or other opinion, national or social origin, property, birth or other status.

2. Where not already provided for by existing legislative or other measures, each State Party to the present

Covenant undertakes to take the necessary steps, in accordance with its constitutional process and with the provisions of the present Covenant, to adopt such legislative or other measures as may be necessary to give effect to the rights recognised in the present Covenant.

3. Each State Party to the present Covenant undertakes:

   (a) To ensure that any person whose rights or freedoms as herein recognised are violated shall have an effective remedy, not-withstanding that the violation has been committed by persons acting in an official capacity;

   (b) To ensure that any person claiming such a remedy shall have his right thereto determined by competent judical, administrative or legislative authorities, or by any other competent authority provided for by the legal system of the State, and to develop the possibilities of judical remedy;

   (c) To ensure that the competent authorities shall enforce such remedies when granted.

Article 3

The States Parties to the present Covenant undertake to ensure the equal right of men and women to the enjoyment of all civil and political rights set forth in the present Covenant.

Article 4

1. In time of public emergency which threatens the life of the nation and the existence of which is officially proclaimed, the States Parties to the present Covenant may take measures derogating from their obligations under the present Covenant to the extent strictly required by the exigencies of the situation, provided that such measures are not inconsistent with their other obligations under international law and do not involve discrimination solely on the ground of race, colour, sex, language, religion or social origin.

2. No derogation from articles 6, 7, 8 (paragraphs 1 and 2), 11, 15, 16 and 18 may be made under this provision.

3. Any State Party to the present Covenant availing itself of the right of derogation shall immediately inform the other States Parties to the present Covenant, through the intermediary of the Secretary-General of the United Nations, of the provisions from which its has derogated and of the reasons by which it was actuated. A further communication shall be made, through the same intermediary, on the date on which it terminates such derogation.

Article 5

1. Nothing in the present Covenant may be interpreted as implying for any State, group or person any right to engage in any activity or perform any act aimed at the destruction of any of the rights and freedoms recognised herein or at their limitation to a greater extent than is provided for in the present Covenant.

2. There shall be no restriction upon or derogation from any of the fundamental human rights recognised or existing in any State Party to the present Covenant pursuant to law, coventions, regulations or custom on the pretext that the present Covenant does not recognise such rights or that it recognises them to a lesser extent.

Part III

Article 6

1. Every human being has the inherent right to life. This right shall be protected by law. No one shall be arbitrarily deprived of his life.

2. In countries which have not abolished the death penalty, sentence of death may be imposed only for the most serious crimes in accordance with the law in force at the time of the commission of the crime and not contrary to the provision of the present Covenant and to the Convention on the Prevention and Punishment of the

Crime of Genocide. This penalty can only be carried out pursuant to a final judgement rendered by a competent court.

3. When deprivation of life constitutes the crime of genocide, it is understood that nothing in this article shall authorise any State Party to the present Covenant to derogate in any way from any obligation assumed under the provisions of the Covention on the Prevention and Punishment of the Crime of Genocide.

4. Anyone sentenced to death shall have the right to seek pardon or commutation of the sentence. Amnesty, pardon or commutation of the sentence of death may be granted in all cases.

5. Sentence of death shall not be imposed for crimes committed by persons below eighteen years of age and shall not be carried out on pregnant women.

6. Nothing in this article shall be invoked to delay or to prevent the abolition of capital punishment by any State Party to the present Covenant.

Article 7

No one shall be subjected to torture or to cruel, inhuman or degrading treatment or punishment. In particular, no one shall be subjected without his free consent to medical or scientific experimentation.

Article 8

1. No one shall be held in slavery; slavery and the slave-trade in all their forms shall be prohibited.

2. No one shall be held in servitude.

3. **(a)** No one shall be required to perform forced or compulsory labour;

   (b) Paragraph 3 (a) shall not be held to preclude, in countries where imprisonment with hard labour may be imposed as a punishment for a crime, the performance of hard labour in pursuance of a sentence to such punishment by a competent court;

(c) For the purpose of this paragraph the term "forced or compulsory labour" shall not include:

(i) Any work or service, not referred to in sub-paragraph (b), normally required of a person who is under detention in consequence of a lawful order of a court, or of a person during conditional release from such detention;

(ii) Any service of a military character and, in countries where conscientious objection is recognised, any national service required by law of conscientious objectors;

(iii) Any service exacted in cases of emergency or calamity threatening the life or well-being of the community;

(iv) Any work or service which forms part of normal civil obligations.

Article 9

1. Everyone has the right to liberty and security of person. No one shall be subjected to arbitrary arrest or detention. No one shall be deprived of his liberty except on such grounds and in accordance with such procedure as are established by law.

2. Anyone who is arrested shall be informed, at the time of arrest, of the reasons for his arrest and shall be promptly informed of any charges against him.

3. Anyone arrested or detained on a criminal charge shall be brought promptly before a judge or other officer authorised by law to exercise judical power and shall be entitled to trial within a reasonable time or to release. It shall not be the general rule that persons awaiting trial shall be detained in custody, but release may be subject to guarantees to appear for trial, at any other stage of the judicial proceedings, and, should occasion arise, for execution of the judgement.

4. Anyone who is deprived of his liberty by arrest or detention shall be entitled to take proceedings before a court, in order that that court may decide without delay on the lawfulness of his detention and order his release if the detention is not lawful.

5. Anyone who has been the victim of unlawful arrest or detention shall have an enforceable right to compensation.

Article 10

1. All persons deprived of their liberty shall be treated with humanity and with respect for the inherent dignity of the human person.

2. **(a)** Accused persons shall, save in exceptional circumstances, be segregated for convicted persons and shall be subject to separate treatment appropriate to their status as unconvicted persons;

   (b) Accused juvenile persons shall be separated from adults and brought as speedily as possible for adjudication.

3. The penitentiary system shall comprise treatment of prisoners the essential aim of which shall be their reformation and social rehabilitation. Juvenile offenders shall be segregated from adults and be accorded treatment appropriate to their age and legal status.

Article 11

No one shall be imprisoned merely on the ground of inability to fulfil a contractual obligation.

Article 12

1. Everyone lawfully within the territory of a State shall, within that territory, have the right to liberty of movement and freedom to choose his residence.

2. Everyone shall be free to leave any country, including his own.

3. The above-mentioned rights shall not be subject to any restrictions except those which are provided by law, are

necessary to protect national security, public order *(ordre public)*, public health or morals or the rights and freedoms of others, and are consistent with the other rights recognised in the present Covenant.

4. No one shall be arbitrarily deprived of the right to enter his own country.

Article 13

An alien lawfully in the territory of a State Party to the present Covenant may be expelled therefrom only in pursuance of a decision reached in accordance with law and shall, except where compelling reasons of national security otherwise require, be allowed to submit the reasons against his expulsion and to have his case reviewed by, and be represented for the purpose before, the competent authority or a person or persons especially designated by the competent authority.

Article 14

1. All persons shall be equal before the courts and tribunals. In the determination of any criminal charge against him, or of his rights and obligations in a suit at law, everyone shall be entitled to a fair and public hearing by a competent, independent and impartial tribunal established by law. The Press and the public may be excluded from all or part of a trial for reasons of morals. Public order *(ordre public)* or national security in a democratic society, or when the interest of the private lives of the parties so requires, or to the extent strictly necessary in the opinion of the court in special circumstances where publicity would prejudice the interests of justice; but any judgement rendered in a criminal case or in a suit at law shall be made public except where the interest of juvenile persons otherwise requires or the proceedings concern matrimonial disputes or the guardianship of children.

2. Everyone charged with a criminal offence shall have the right to be presumed innocent until proved guilty according to law.

3. In the determination of any criminal charge against him, everyone shall be entitled to the following minimum guarantees, in full equality:

   (a) To be informed promptly and in detail in a language which he understands of the nature and cause of the charge against him;

   (b) To have adequate time and facilities for the preparation of his defence and to communicate with counsel of his own choosing;

   (c) To be tried without undue delay;

   (d) To be tried in his presence, and to defend himself in person or through legal assistance of his own choosing; to be informed, if he does not have legal assistance, of this right; and to have legal assistance assigned to him, in any case where the interests of justice so require, and without payment by him in any such case if he does not have sufficient means to pay for it;

   (e) To examine, or have examined, the witnesses against him and to obtain the attendance and examination of witnesses on his behalf under the same conditions as witnesses against him;

   (f) To have the free assistance of an interpreter if he cannot understand or speak the language used in court;

   (g) Not to be compelled to testify against himself or to confess guilt.

4. In the case of juvenile persons, the procedure shall be such as will take account of their age and the desirability or promoting their rehabilitation.

5. Everyone convicted of a crime shall have the right to his conviction and sentence being reviewed by a higher tribunal according to law.

6. When a person has by a final decision been convicted of a criminal offence and when subsequently his conviction

has been reversed or he has been pardoned on the ground that a new or newly discovered fact shows conclusively that there has been a miscarriage of justice, the person who has suffered punishment as a result of such conviction shall be compensated according to law, unless it is proved that the non-disclosure of the unknown fact, in time is wholly or partly attributable to him.

7. No one shall be liable to be tried or punished again for an offence for which he has already been finally convicted or acquitted in accordance with the law and penal procedure of each country.

Article 15

1. No one shall be held guilty of any criminal offence on account of any act or omission which did not constitute a criminal offence, under national or international law, at the time when it was committed. Nor shall a heavier penalty be imposed than the one that was applicable at the time when the criminal offence was committed. If, subsequent to the commission of the offence, provision is made by law for the imposition of a lighter penalty, the offender shall benefit thereby.

2. Nothing in this article shall prejudice the trial and punishment of any person for any act or omission which, at the time when it was committed, was criminal according to the general principles of law recognised by the community of nations.

Article 16

Everyone shall have the right to recognition everywhere as a person before the law.

Article 17

1. No one shall be subjected to arbitrary or unlawful interference with his privacy, family, home or correspondence, nor to unlawful attacks on his honour and reputation.

2. Everyone has the right to the protection of the law against such interference or attacks.

Article 18

1. Everyone shall have the right to freedom of thought, conscience and religion. This right shall include freedom to have or to adopt a religion or belief of his choice, and freedom, either individually or in community with others and in public or private, to manifest his religion or belief in worship, observance, practice and teaching.

2. No one shall be subject to coercion which would impair his freedom to have or to adopt a religion or belief of his choice.

3. Freedom to manifest one's religion or beliefs may be subject only to such limitations as are prescribed by law and are necessary to protect public safety, order, health or morals or the fundamental rights and freedoms of others.

4. The States Parties to the present Covenant undertake to have respect for the liberty of parents and, when applicable, legal guardians to ensure the religious and moral education of their children in conformity with their own convictions.

Article 19

1. Everyone shall have the right to hold opinions without interference.

2. Everyone shall have the right to freedom of expression; this right shall include freedom to seek, receive and impart information and ideas of all kinds, regardless of frontiers, either orally, in writing or in print, in the form of art, or through any other media of his choice.

3. The exercise of the rights provided for in paragraph 2 of this article carries with it special duties and responsibilities. It may therefore be subject to certain restrictions, but these shall only be such as are provided by a law and are necessary:

   (a) For respect of the rights or reputations of others;

   (b) For the protection of national security or of public order *(ordre public)*, or of public health or morals.

Article 20

1. Any propaganda for war shall be prohibited by law.

2. Any advocacy of national, racial or religious hatred that constitutes incitement to discrimination, hostility or violence shall be prohibited by law.

Article 21

The right of peaceful assembly shall be recognised. No restrictions may be placed on the exercise of this right other than those imposed in conformity with the law and which are necessary in a democratic society in the interest of national security or public safety, public order *(ordre public),* the protection of public health or morals or the protection of the rights and freedoms of others.

Article 22

1. Everyone shall have the right to freedom of association with others, including the right to form and join trde unions for the protection of his interests.

2. No restrictions may he placed on the exercise of this right other than those which are prescribed by law and which are necessary in a democratic society in the interests of national security or public safety, public order *(ordre public),* the protection of public health or morals or the protection of the rights and freedoms of others. This article shall not prevent the imposition of lawful restrictions on members of the armed forces and of the police in their exercise of this right.

3. Nothing in this article shall authorise States Parties to the International Labour Organisation Convention of 1948 concerning Freedom of Association and Protection of the Right to Organise to take legislative measures which would prejudice, or to apply the law in such a manner as to prejudice, the guarantees provided for in that Covention.

Article 23

1. The family is the natural and fundamental group unit of society and is entitled to protection by society and the State.

2. The right of men and women of marriageable age to marry and to found a family shall be recognised.

3. No marriage shall be entered into without the free and full consent of the intending spouses.

4. States Parties to the present Covenant shall take appropriate steps to ensure equality or rights and responsibilities of spouses as to marriage, during marriage and at its dissolution. In the case of dissolution, provision shall be made for the necessary protection of any children.

Article 24

1. Every child shall have, without any discrimination as to race, colour, sex, language, religion, national of social origin, property or birth, the right to such measures of protection as are required by his status as a minor, on the part of his family, society and the State.

2. Every child shall be registered immediately after birth and shall have a name.

3. Every child has the right to acquire a nationality.

Article 25

Every citizen shall have the right and the opportunity, without any of the distinctions mentioned in article 2 and without unreasonable restrictions:

(a) To take part in the conduct of public affairs, directly or through freely chosen representatives;

(b) To vote and to be elected at genuine periodic elections which shall be by universal and equal suffrage and shall be held by secret ballot, guaranteeing the free expression of the will of the electors;

(c) To have access, on general terms of equality, to public service in his country;

Article 26

All persons are equal before the law and are entitled without any discrimination to the equal protection of the law.

In this respect, the law shall prohibit any discrimination and guarantee to all persons equal and effective protection against discrimination on any ground such as race, colour, sex, language, religion, political or other opinion, national or social origin, property, birth or other status.

Article 27

In those States in which ethnic, religious or linguistic minorities exist, persons belonging to such minorities shall not be denied the right, in community with the other members of their group, to enjoy their own culture, to profess and practise their own religion, or to use their own language.

Part IV

Article 28

1. There shall be established a Human Rights Committee (hereafter referred to in the present Covenant as the Committee). It shall consist of eighteen members and shall carry out the functions hereinafter provided.

2. The Committee shall be composed of nationals of the States Parties to the present Covenant who shall be persons of high moral character and recognised competence in the field of human rights, consideration being given to the usefulness of the participation of some persons having legal experience.

3. The members of the Committee shall be elected and shall serve in their personal capacity.

Article 29

1. The members of the Committee shall be elected by secret ballot from a list of persons possessing the qualifications prescribed in article 28 and nominated for the purpose by the States Parties to the present Covenant.

2. Each State Party to the present Covenant may nominate not more than two persons. These persons shall be nationals of the nominating State.

3. A person shall be eligible for renomination.

Article 30

1. The initial election shall be held no later than six months after the date of the entry into force of the present Covenant.
2. At least four months before the date of each election to the Committee, other than an election to fill a vacancy declared in according with article 34, the Secretary-General of the United Nations shall address a written invitation to the States Parties to the present Covenant to submit their nominations for membership of the Committee within three months.
3. The Secretary-General of the United Nations shall prepare a list in alphabetical order of all the persons thus nominated, with an indication of the States Parties which have nominated them, and shall submit it to the States Parties to the present Covenant no later than one month before the date of each election.
4. Elections of the members of the Committee shall be held at a meeting of the States Parties to the present Covenant convened by the Secretary-General of the United Nations at the Headquarters of the United Nations. At that meeting, for which two thirds of the States Parties to the present Covenant shall constitute a quorum, the persons elected to the Committee shall be those nominees who obtain the largest number of votes and an absolute majority of the votes of the representatives of States Parties present and voting.

Article 31

1. The Committee may not include more than one national of the same State.
2. In the election of the Committee, consideration shall be given to equitable geographical distribution of membership and to the representation of the different forms of civilisation and of the principal legal systems.

Article 32

1. The members of the Committee shall be elected for a term of four years. They shall be eligible for re-election

if renominated. However, the terms of nine of the members elected at the first election shall expire at the end of two years; immediately after the first election, the names of these nine members shall be chosen by lot by the Chairman of the meeting referred to in article 30, paragraph 4.

2. Elections at the expiry of office shall be held in accordance with the preceding articles of this part of the present Covenant.

Article 33

1. If, in the unanimous opinion of the other members, a member of the Committee has ceased to carry out his functions for any cause other than absence of a temporary character, the Chairman of the Committee shall notify the Secretary-General of the United Nations, who shall then declare the seat of that member to be vacant.

2. In the event of the death or the resignation of a member of the Committee, the Chairman shall immediately notify the Secretary-General of the United Nations, who shall declare the seat vacant from the date of death or the date on which the resignation takes effect.

Article 34

1. When a vacancy is declared in accordance with article 33 and if the term of office of the member to be replaced does not expire within six months of the declaration of the vacancy, the Secretary General of the United Nations shall notify each of the States Parties to the present Covenant which may within two months submit nominations in accordance with article 29 for the purpose of filling the vacancy.

2. The Secretary-General of the United Nations shall prepare a list in alphabetical order of the persons thus nominated and shall submit it to the States Parties to the present Covenant. The election to fill the vacancy shall then take place in accordance with the relevant provisions of this part of the present Covenant.

3. A member of the Committee elected to fill a vacancy declared in accordance with article 33 shall hold office for the remainder of the term of the member who vacated the seat on the Committee under the provisions of that article.

Article 35

The members of the Committee shall, with the approval of the General Assembly of the United Nations, receive emoluments from United Nations resources on such terms and conditions as the General Assembly may decide, having regard to the importance of the Committee's responsibilities.

Article 36

The Secretary-General of the United Nations shall provide the necessary staff and facilities for the effective performance of the functions of the Committee under the present Covenant.

Article 37

1. The Secretary-General of the United Nations shall convene the initial meeting of the Committee at the Headquarters of the United Nations.
2. After its initial meeting, the Committee shall meet at such times as shall be provided in its rules of procedure.
3. The Committee shall normally meet at the Headquarters of the United Nations or at the United Nations Office at Geneva.

Article 38

Every member of the Committee shall, before taking up his duties, make a solemn declaration in open committee that he will perform his functions impartially and conscientiously.

Article 39

1. The Committee shall elect its officers for a term of two years. They may be re-elected.
2. The Committee shall establish its own rules of procedure, but these rules shall provide, *inter alia,* that:

(a) Twelve members shall constitute a quorum;

(b) Decisions of the Committee shall be made by a majority vote of the members present.

Article 40

1. The States Parties to the present Covenant undertake to submit reports on the measures they have adopted which give effect to the rights recognised herein and on the progress made in the enjoyment of those rights:

   (a) Within one year of the entry into force of the present Covenant for the States Parties concerned;

   (b) Thereafter whenever the Committee so requests.

2. All reports shall be submitted to the Secretary-General of the United Nations, who shall transmit them to the Committee for consideration. Reports shall indicate the factors and difficulties, if any, affecting the implementation of the present Covenant.

3. The Secretary-General of the United Nations may, after consultation with the Committee, transmit to the specialised agencies concerned copies of such parts of the reports as may fall within their field of competence.

4. The Committee shall study the reports submitted by the States Parties to the Covenant. It shall transmit its reports, and such general comments as it may consider appropriate, to the States Parties. The Committee may also transmit to the Economic and Social Council these comments along with the copies of the reports it has received from States Parties to the present Covenant.

5. The States Parties to the present Covenant may submit to the Committee observations on any comments that may be made in accordance with paragraph 4 of this article.

Article 41

1. A State Party to the present Covenant may at any time declare under this article that it recognises the competence of the Committee to receive and consider

communications to the effect that a State Party claims that another State Party is not fulfilling its obligations under the present Covenant. Communications under this article may be received and considered only if submitted by a State Party which has made a declaration recognizing in regard to itself the competence of the Committee. No communication shall be received by the Committee if it concerns a State Party which has not made such a declaration. Communications received under this article shall be dealt with in accordance with the following procedure:

(a) If a State Party to the present Covenant considers that another State Party is not giving effect to the provisions of the present Covenant, it may, by written communication, bring the matter to the attention of that State Party. Within three months after the receipt of the communication, the receiving State shall afford the State which sent the communication an explanation or any other statement in writing clarifying the matter, which should include, to the extent possible and pertinent, reference to domestic procedures and remedies taken, pending, or available in the matter.

(b) If the matter is not adjusted to the satisfaction of both States Parties concerned within six months after the receipt by the receiving State of the initial communication, either State shall have the right to refer the matter to the Committee, by notice given to the Committee and to the other State.

(c) The Committee shall deal with the matter referred to it only after it has ascertained that all available domestic remedies have been invoked and exhausted in the matter, in conformity with the generally recognised principles of international law. This shall not be the rule where the application of the remedies is unreasonably prolonged.

(d) The Committee shall hold closed meetings when examining communications under this article.

(e) Subject to the provisions of sub-paragraph (c), the Committee shall make available its good offices to the States Parties concerned with a view to a friendly solution of the matter on the basis of respect for human rights and fundamental freedoms as recognised in the present Covenant.

(f) In any matter referred to it, the Committee may call upon the States Parties concerned, referred to in sub-paragraph (b), to supply any relevant information.

(g) The States Parties concerned, referred to in sub-paragraph (b), shall have the right to be represented when the matter is being considered in the Committee and to make submissions orally and/or in writing.

(h) The Committee shall, within twelve months after the date of receipt of notice under sub-paragraph (b), submit a report:

(i) If a solution within the terms of sub-paragraph (e) is reached, the Committee shall confine its report to a brief statement of the facts and of the solution reached;

(ii) If a solution within the terms of sub-paragraph (e) is not reached, the Committee shall confine its report to a brief statement of the facts; the written submissions and record of the oral submissions made by he State parties concerned shall be attached to the report.

In every matter, the report shall be communicated to the States Parties concerned.

2. The provisions of this article shall come into force when ten States parties to the present Covenant have made declarations under paragraph 1 of this article. Such

declarations shall be deposited by the States Parties with the Secretary-General of the United Nations, who shall transmit copies thereof to the other States Parties. A declaration may be withdrawn at any time by notification to the Secretary-General. Such a withdrawal shall not prejudice the consideration of any matter which is the subject of a communication already transmitted under this article; no further communication by any State Party shall be received after the notification of withdrawal of the declaration has been received by the Secretary-General, unless the State Party concerned had made a new declaration.

Article 42

1. **(a)** If a matter referred to the Committee in accordance with article 41 is not resolved to the satisfaction of the States Parties concerned, the Committee may, with the prior consent of the States Parties concerned, appoint an *ad hoc* Conciliation Commission (hereinafter referred to as the Commission). The good offices of the Commission shall be made available to the States Parties concerned with a view to an amicable solution of the matter on the basis of respect for the present Covenant;

   (b) The Commission shall consist of five persons acceptable to the States Parties concerned. If the States Parties concerned fail to reach agreement within three months on all or part of the composition of the Commission, the members of the Commission concerning whom no agreement has been reached shall be elected by secret ballot by a two-thirds majority vote of the committee from among its members.

2. The members of the Commission shall serve in their personal capacity. They shall not be nationals of the States Parties concerned, or of a State not party to the present Covenant, or of a State Party which has not made a declaration under article 41.

3. The Commission shall elect its own Chairman adn adopt its own rules of procedure.

4. The meetings of the Commission shall normally be held at the Headquarters of the United Nations or at the United Nations Office at Geneva. However, they may be held at such other convenient places as the Commission may determine in consultation with the Secretary-General of the United Nations and the States Parties concerned.

5. The secretariat provided in accordance with article 36 shall also service the commissions appointed under this article.

6. The information received and collated by the Committee shall be made available to the Commission and the Commission may call upon the States parties concerned to supply any other relevant information.

7. When the Commission has fully considered the matter, but in any event not later than twelve months after having been seized of the matter, it shall submit to the Chairman of the Committee a report for communication to the State Parties concerned:

   (a) If the Commission is unable to complete its consideration of the matter within twelve months, it shall confine its report to a brief statement of the status of its consideration of the matter;

   (b) If an amicable solution to the matter on the basis of respect for human rights as recognised in the present Covenant is reached, the Commission shall confine its report to a brief statement of the facts and of the solution reached;

   (c) If a solution within the terms of sub-paragraph (b) is not reached, the Commission's report shall embody its findings on all questions of fact relevant to the issues between the States Parties concerned, and its views on the possibilities of an amicable solution of the matter. This report shall also contain the written submissions and a record of the oral submissions made by the States parties concerned;

(d) If the Commission's report is submitted under sub-paragraph (c), the States Parties concerned shall, within three months of the receipt of the report, notify the Chairman of the Committee whether or not they accept the contents of the report of the Commission.

8. The provisions of this article are without prejudice to the responsibilities of the Committee under article 41.

9. The States Parties concerned shall share equally all the expenses of the members of the Commission in accordance with estimates to be provided by the Secretary-General of the United Nations.

10. The Secretary-General of the United Nations shall be empowered to pay the expenses of the members of the Commission, if necessary before reimbursement by the States Parties concerned, in accordance with paragraph 9 of this article.

Article 43

The members of the Committee, and of the *ad hoc* conciliation commissions which may be appointed under article 42, shall be entitled to the facilities, privileges and immunities of experts on mission for the United Nations as laid down in the relevant sections of the Convention of the Privileges and Immunities of the United Nations.

Article 44

The provisions for the implementation of the present Covenant shall apply without prejudice to the procedures prescribed in the field of human rights by or under the constituent instruments and the conventions of the United Nations and of the specialised agencies and shall not prevent the States Parties to the present Covenant from having recourse to other procedures for settling a dispute in accordance with general or special international agreements in force between them.

Article 45

The Committee shall submit to the General Assembly of the United Nations, through the Economic and Social Council, an annual report on its activities.

Part V

Article 46

Nothing in the present Covenant shall be interpreted as impairing the provisions of the Charter of the United Nations and of the constitutions of the specialised agencies which define the respective responsibilities of the various organs of the United Nations and of the specialised agencies in regard to the matters dealt with in the present Covenant.

Article 47

Nothing in the present Covenant shall be interpreted as impairing the inherent right of all peoples to enjoy and utilise fully and freely their natural wealth and resources.

Part VI

Article 48

1. The present Covenant is open for signature by any State Member of the United Nations or member of any of its specialised agencies, by any State Party to the Statute of the International Court of Justice, and by any other State which has been invited by the General Assembly of the United Nations to become a party to the present Covenant.

2. The present Covenant is subject to ratification. Instruments of ratification shall be deposited with the Secretary-General or the United Nations.

3. The present Covenant shall be open to accession by any State referred to in paragraph 1 of this article.

4. Accession shall be effected by the deposit of an instrument of accession with the Secretary-General of the United Nations.

5. The Secretary-General of the United Nations shall inform all States which have signed this Covenant or acceded to it of the deposit of each instrument of ratification or accession.

Article 49

1. The present Covenant shall enter into force three months after the date of the deposit with the Secretary-General of the United Nations of the thirty-fifth instrument of ratification or instrument of accession.
2. For each State ratifying the present Covenant or acceding to it after the deposit of the thirty-fifth instrument of ratification or instrument of accession, the present Covenant shall enter into force three months after the date of the deposit of its own instrument of ratification or instrument of accession.

Article 50

The provisions of the present Covenant shall extend to all parts of federal States without any limitations or exceptions.

Article 51

1. Any State Party to the present Covenant may propose an amendment and file it with the Secretary-General of the United Nations. The Secretary-General of the United Nations shall thereupon communicate any proposed amendments to the States Parties to the present Covenant with a request that they notify him whether they favour a conference of States Parties for the purpose of considering and voting upon the proposals. In the event that at least one third of the States Parties favours such a conference, the Secretary General shall converse the conference under the auspices of the United Nations. Any amendment adopted by a majority of the States Parties present and voting at the conference shall be submitted to the General Assembly of the United Nations for approval.
2. Amendments shall come into force when they have been approved by the General Assembly of the United Nations

and accepted by a two-thirds majority of the States Parties to the Present Covenant in accordance with their respective constitutional processes.

3. When amendments come into force, they shall be binding on those States Parties which have accepted them, other States Parties still being bound by the provisions of the present Covenant and any earlier amendment which they have accepted.

Article 52

Irrespective of the notifications made under article 48, paragraph 5, the Secretary-General of the United Nations shall inform all States referred to in paragraph 1 of the same article of the following particulars:

(a) Signatures, ratifications and accessions under article 48;

(b) The date of the entry into force of the present Covenant under article 49 and the date of the entry into force of any amendments under article 51.

Article 53

1. The present Covenant of which the Chinese, English, French, Russian and Spanish texts are equally authentic, shall be deposited in the archives of the United Nations.

2. The Secretary-General of the United Nations shall transmit certified copies of the present Covenant to all States referred to in article 48.

OPTIONAL PROTOCOL TO THE INTERNATIONAL COVENANT ON CIVIL AND POLITICAL RIGHTS

The States Parties to the Present Protocol,

Considering that in order further to achieve the purposes of the Covenant on Civil and Political Rights (hereinafter referred to as the Covenant) and the implementation of its provisions it would be appropriate to enable the Human Rights Committee set up in part IV of the Covenant (hereinafter referred to as the Committee) to receive and consider, as provided in the present Protocol, communications from individuals claiming to be victims of violations of any of the rights set forth in the Covenant,

Have agreed as follows:

Article 1

A State Party to the Covenant that becomes a party to the present Protocol recognises the competence of the Committee to receive and consider communications from individuals subject to its jurisdiction who claim to be victims of a violation by that State Party of any of the rights set forth in the Covenant. No communication shall be received by the Committee if it concerns a State Party to the Covenant which is not a party to the present Protocol.

Article 2

Subject to the provisions of article 1, individuals who claim that any of their rights enumerated in the Covenant have been violated and who have exhausted all available domestic remedies may submit a written communication to the Committee for consideration.

Article 3

The Committee shall consider inadmissible any communication under the present Protocol which is anonymous, or which it considers to be an abuse of the rights of submission of such communications or to be incompatible with the provisions of the Covenant.

Article 4

1. Subject to the provisions of article 3, the Committee shall bring any communications submitted to it under the present Protocol to the attention of the State Party to the present Protocol alleged to be violating any provisions of the Covenant.

2. Within six months, the receiving State shall submit to the Committee written explanations or statements clarifying the matter and the remedy, if any, that may have been taken by that State.

Article 5

1. The Committee shall consider communications received under the present Protocol in the light of all written information made available to it by the individual and by the State Party concerned.

2. The Committee shall not consider any communication from an individual unless it has ascertained that:

   (a) The same matter is not being examined under another procedure of international investigation or settlement;

   (b) The individual has exhausted all available domestic remedies. This shall not be the rule where the application of the remedies is unreasonably prolonged.

   3. The Committee shall hold closed meetings when examining communications under the present Protocol.

   4. The Committee shall forward its views to the State Party concerned and to the individual.

Article 6

The Committee shall include in its annual report under article 45 of the Covenant a summary of its activities under the present Protocol.

Article 7

Pending the achievement of the objectives of resolution 1514 (XV) adopted by the General Assembly of the United nations on 14 December 1960 concerning the Declaration on the Granting of Independence to Colonial Countries and Peoples, the provisions of the present Protocol shall in no way limit the right of petition granted to these peoples by the Charter of the United Nations and other international conventions and instruments under the United Nations and its specialised agencies.

Article 8

1. The present Protocol is open for signature by any State which has signed the Covenant.

2. The present Protocol is subject to ratification by any State which has ratified or acceded to the Covenant. Instruments of ratification shall be deposited with the Secretary-General of the United Nations.

3. The present Protocol shall be open to accession by any State which has ratified or acceded to the Covenant.

4. Accession shall be effected by the deposit of an instrument of accession with the Secretary-General of the United Nations

5. The Secretary-General of the United Nations shall inform all States which have signed the present Protocol or acceded to it of the deposit of each instrument of ratification or accession.

Article 9

1. Subject to the entry into force of the Covenant, the present Protocol shall enter into force three months after the date of the deposit with the Secretary-General of the United Nations of the tenth instrument of ratification or instrument of accession.

2. For each State ratifying the present Protocol or acceding to it after the deposit of the tenth instrument of ratification or instrument of accession, the present Protocol shall enter into force three months after the date of the deposit of its own instrument of ratification or instrument of accession.

Article 10

The provisions of the present Protocol shall extend to all parts of federal States without any limitations or exceptions.

Article 11

1. Any State Party to the present Protocol may propose an amendment and file it with the Secretary-General of the United Nations.

The Secretary-General shall thereupon communicate any proposed amendments to the States Parties to the present protocol with a request that they notify him whether they favour a conference of States Parties for the purpose of considering and voting upon the proposal. In the event that at least one third of the States Parties favours such a conference, the Secretary-General shall convene the conference under the auspices of the United Nations. Any amendment adopted by a majority of the States Parties present and voting at the conference shall be submitted to the General Assembly of the United Nations for approval.

2. Amendments shall come into force when they have been approved by the General Assembly of the United Nations and accepted by a two-thirds majority of the States Parties to the present Protocol in accordance with their respective constitutional processes.

3. When amendments come into force, they shall be binding on those States Parties which have accepted them, other States Parties still being bound by the provisions of the present Protocol and any earlier amendment which they have accepted.

Article 12

1. Any State Party may denounce the present Protocol at any time by written notification addressed to the Secretary-General of the United Nations. Denunciation shall take effect three months are the date of receipt of the notification by the Secretary-General.

2. Denunciation shall be without prejudice to the continued application of the provisions of the present Protocol to any communication submitted under article 2 before the effective date of denunciation.

Article 13

Irrespective of the notifications made under article 8, paragraph 5, of the present Protocol, the Secretary-General of the United Nations shall inform all State referred to in article 48, paragraph 1, of the Covenant of the following particulars:

(a) Signatures, ratifications and accessions under article 8;

(b) The date of the entry into force of any amendments under article 11;

(c) Denunciations under article 12.

Article 14

1. The present Protocol, of which the Chinese, English, French, Russian and Spanish texts are equally authentic, shall be deposited in the archives of the United Nations.

2. The Secretary-General of the United Nations shall transmit certified copies of the present Protocol to all States referred to in article 48 of the Covenant.

SECOND OPTIONAL PROTOCOL TO THE INTERNATIONAL COVENANT ON CIVIL AND POLITICAL RIGHTS AIMING AT THE ABOLITION OF THE DEATH PENALTY

The state parties to the present protocol,

Believing that abolition of the death penalty contributes to enhancement of human dignity and progressive development of human rights,

Recalling article 3 of the Universal Declaration of Human Rights adopted on 10 December 1948 and article 6 of the International Covenant on Civil and Political Rights adopted on 16 December 1966,

Noting that article 6 of the International Covenant on Civil and Political Rights refers to abolition of the death penalty in terms that strongly suggest that abolition is desirable,

Convinced that all measures of abolition of the death penalty should be considered as progress in the enjoyment of the right to life,

Desirous to undertake hereby an international commitment to abolish the death penalty,

Have agreed as follows:

Article 1

1. No one within the jurisdiction of the State Party to the present Protocol shall be executed.

2. Each State Party shall take all necessary measures to abolish the death penalty within its jurisdiction.

Article 2

1. No reservation is admissible to the present Protocol, except for a reservation made at the time of ratification or accession that provides for the application of the death penalty in time of war pursuant to a conviction for a most serious crime of a military nature committed during wartime.

2. The State Party making such a reservation shall at the time of ratification or accession communicate to the Secretary-General of the United Nations the relevant provisions of its national legislation applicable during wartime.

3. The State Party having made such a reservation shall notify the Secretary-General of the United Nations of any beginning or ending of a state of war applicable to its territory.

Article 3

The States Parties to the present Protocol shall include in the reports they submit to the Human Rights Committee, in accordance with article 40 of the Covenant, information on the measures that they have adopted to give effect to the present Protocol.

Article 4

With respect to the States Parties to the Covenant that have made a declaration under article 41, the competence of the human Rights Committee to receive and consider communications when a State Party claims that another State party is not fulfilling its obligations shall extend to the provisions of the present Protocol, unless the State Party concerned has made a statement to the contrary at the moment of ratification or accession.

Article 5

With respect to the States Parties to the first optional Protocol to the International Covenant on Civil and Political

Rights adopted on 16 December 1966, the competence of the Human Rights Committee to receive and consider communications from individuals subject to its jurisdiction shall extend to the provisions of the present Protocol, unless the State Party concerned has made a statement to the contrary at the moment of rectification or accession.

Article 6

1. The provisions of the present Protocol shall apply as additional provisions to the Covenant.

2. Without prejudice to the possibility of a reservation under article 2 of the present Protocol, the right guaranteed in article 1, paragraph 1, of the present Protocol shall not be subject to any derogation under article 4 of the Covenant.

Article 7

1. The present Protocol is open for signature by any State that has signed the Covenant.

2. The present Protocol is subject to ratification by any State that has ratified the Covenant or acceded to it. Instruments of ratification shall be deposited with the Secretary-General of the United Nations.

3. The present Protocol shall be open to accession by any State that has ratified the Covenant or acceded to it.

4. Accession shall be effected by the deposit of an instrument of accession with the Secretary-General of the United Nations.

5. The Secretary-General of the United Nations shall inform all States that have signed the present Protocol or acceded to it of the deposit of each instrument of ratification or accession.

Article 8

1. The present Protocol shall enter into force three months after the date of the deposit with the Secretary-General of the United Nations of the tenth instrument of ratification or accession.

2. For each State ratifying the present Protocol or acceding to it after the deposit of the tenth instrument of ratification or accession, the present Protocol shall enter into force three months after the date of the deposit of its own instrument of ratification or accession.

Article 9

The provision of the present Protocol shall extend to all parts of federal States without any limitations or exceptions.

Article 10

The Secretary-General of the United Nations shall inform all States referred to in article 48, paragraph 1, of the Covenant of the following particulars:

(a) Reservations, communications and notifications under article 2 of the present Protocol;

(b) Statements made under articles 4 or 5 of the present Protocol;

(c) Signatures, ratifications and accessions under article 7 of the present Protocol.

(d) The date of the entry into force of the present Protocol under article 8 thereof.

Article 11

1. The present protocol, of which the Arabic, Chinese, English, French, Russian and Spanish texts are equally authentic, shall be deposited in the archives of the United Nations.

2. The Secretary-General of the United Nations shall transmit certified copies of the present Protocol to all States referred to in article 48 of the Covenant.

Annex II

HUMAN RIGHTS A UNITED NATIONS PRIORITY

Introduction

We are Living in an era of Dramatic Change and transition, in a world that is being transformed by complex financial systems and revolutionary information technologies into a vast global marketplace. Globalisation is creating new patterns of interaction among people and States, promising unprecedented opportunities for material progress in larger freedom, but also threatening to compound many existing challengers before the international community while deepening the economic marginalisation of those most vulnerable. In this complex scenario, human rights, which were embedded formally at the United Nations as a great international priority 50 years ago—through the December 1948 Universal Declaration of Human Rights—have gained prominence as a universally recognised set of norms and standards that increasingly inform all aspects of our relations as individuals and as collective members of groups, within communities and among nations. There is now near-universal recognition that respect for human rights—the rights of political choice and association, of opinion and expression, and of culture; the freedom from fear and from all forms of discrimination and prejudice; freedom from want and the right to employment and well-being and, collectively, to development—is essential to the sustainable achievement of the three agreed global priorities of peace, development and democracy.

Given their centrality, the United Nations has made the strengthening of human rights a crosscutting focus in all its work. But assuring human rights for all people remains a daunting challenge, especially given the impunity with which they continue to be violated in all parts of the world. Billions continue to live in extreme poverty, and the huge disparity between rich and poor countries continues to grow. Violent conflicts, increasingly ethnic in nature, have proliferated, uprooting entire communities, forcing millions of people from their homes. Political extremism and terrorism continue to target countless innocent civilians. Unemployment, discrimination and social exclusion bedevil all societies. And although globalisation has brought the world closer together, it has also benefited elements of uncivil society, reflected in the increase in corruption, organised crime and transnational trafficking in illicit drugs, arms, toxic materials, even in human beings, particularly of women for sexual exploitation.

The revitalisation of the United Nations that has become another priority in recent years will be judged in large part by its success in meeting these challenges—old and new—and in extending not merely the theory but the practice of human rights. The first-ever judgements and sentencing for the crime of genocide—50 years after the Convention on Genocide was concluded—by the International Criminal Tribunal for Rwanda in September 1998, and the agreement in Rome two months previously, on the establishment of an international Criminal Court, are concrete examples of a deepened resolve by the international community to ensure respect for all human rights, and of the centrality of the Untied Nations and its effectiveness in the realisation of this goal.

Today's United Nations human rights programme has evolved in over 50 years of difficult but steady progress in the face of numerous challenges and frequent disappointments. Since its creation in 1945, the United Nations has overseen the codification of human rights in a major effort to move them from the realm of ethical guidelines to that of binding law. Especially, the Universal Declaration of Human Rights, adopted in 1948, continues to guide the United Nations through the simplicity of its language and the clarity of its purpose. The Universal Declaration, and eloquent inspiration for the worldwide struggle for human dignity and freedom, has become the cornerstone of an increasingly cohesive body of international human rights standards and laws. The enhanced focus on human rights is, in turn, having a direct impact on all aspects of the work of the United Nations, in many cases, such as the role and rights of women, driving action in crucial areas.

This part of the book describes the manifold aspects of United Nations work in the area of human rights today, and the challenges that lie ahead in realizing the objectives of the body of human rights law now in place. The Organisation bases its work on the principle that human rights are universal and indivisible. In practical terms, this means that all rights and freedoms—economic rights, as well as political and civil freedoms—are interrelated and interdependent, and need to be promoted and protected in equal manner. If one set of rights is promoted at the expense of another, then all rights are undermined. For this reason, the Untied Nations has sought a balanced and comprehensive approach to the effective promotion of all human rights, including the right to development. Overcoming the artificial split between two "kinds" of rights is the key to an overall promotion of human rights.

Another common thread in United Nations human rights action is to challenge discrimination in all its forms. It has a long history of fighting racism and racial discrimination and, in recent years, it has increasingly focused on the widespread discrimination against ethnic, religious or linguistic minorities, as well as on the basis of gender. It has stepped up efforts to protect vulnerable groups, such as indigenous people, migrant workers and especially children, who are the most vulnerable to physical and sexual exploitation, particularly in times of armed conflict. The United Nations also continues to work for the advancement and empowerment of women in society, and combats all forms of discrimination and violence against women and girls, whether in private or in public life.

The United Nations is increasingly integrating a human rights component into its peacekeeping operations and into its humanitarian activities, as well as advocating a rights-based approach to peace-building in the aftermath of conflicts. For the United Nations, conflict prevention also means fighting impunity, ensuring that the perpetrators of the most atrocious violations of human rights—genocide, war crimes and crimes against humanity—are held accountable for their offences. This is the main rationale for the international criminal tribunals for Rwanda and the former Yugoslavia and for the recent decision to establish a permanent International Criminal Court, which will have its seat at The Hague in the Netherlands.

With the standard-setting work in international human rights law nearly complete, the United Nations is now concentrating efforts and marshalling resources to implement the legislation. The Organisation seeks to ensure the compliance of Member States and to effectively promote a global culture of human rights through a number of practical strategies:

- Various working groups and experts advance human rights research, establishing standards, codifying the content of human rights, identifying obstacles to their implementation and developing ways to realise these rights;
- An evolving human rights monitoring system of commissions and committees responds to growing demands to prevent or remedy human rights violations, pressing for the universal ratification of international human rights treaties and assisting Governments in conforming to the provisions of these treaties; and
- A growing number of technical cooperation and training programmes in the administration of justice, implemented through human rights field operations and offices, assist States and civil society worldwide in building national networks supporting and strengthening human rights and the rule of law at regional and local levels.

The United Nations continues to reorient its human rights programme to respond more effectively to today's challenges, whether they arise as massive human rights violations or systematic political oppression or persist in more complex and pervasive forms of discrimination—affecting the right to development or the right to a healthy environment, for example. However, it is internationally recognised that the prime responsibility for the promotion and protection of human rights remains with Member States. For this reason, in order to strengthen human rights at the national level, the United Nations has greatly expanded its human rights work in the field. Through the Office of the United Nations High Commissioner for Human Rights, the focal point of all system-wide integration of human rights activities, the United Nations assists Governments and other national and international partners in their promotion and protection of human rights. Strengthening international human rights law and increasing accountability of individuals and Member States in the area of human rights are crucial steps towards an effective implementation of human rights standards. All these complementary approaches advance and enhance United Nations efforts to create a global culture of human rights.

UNIVERSAL DECLARATION OF HUMAN RIGHTS

Fifty years ago, the United Nations General Assembly adopted the Universal Declaration of Human Rights as a bulwark against oppression and discrimination. In the wake of a devastating world war, which had witnessed some of the most barbarous crimes in human history, the Universal Declaration marked the first time that the rights and freedoms of individuals were set forth in such detail. It also represented the first international recognition that human rights and fundamental freedoms are applicable to every person, everywhere. In this sense the Universal Declaration was a landmark achievement in world history. Today, it continues to affect people's lives and inspire human rights activism and legislation all over the world.

The Universal Declaration is remarkable in two fundamental aspects. In 1948, the then 58 Member States of the United Nations represented a range of ideologies, political systems and religious and cultural backgrounds, as well as different stages of economic development. The authors of the Declaration, themselves from different regions of the world, sought to ensure that the draft text would reflect these different cultural traditions and incorporate common values inherent in the world's principal legal systems and religious and philosophical traditions. Most important, the Universal Declaration was to be a common statement of mutual aspirations—a shared vision of a more equitable and just world.

The success of their endeavour is demonstrated by the virtually universal acceptance of the Declaration. Today, the Universal Declaration, translated into nearly 250 national and local languages, is the best known and most cited human rights document in the world. The foundation of international human rights law, the Universal Declaration serves as a model for numerous international treaties and declarations and is incorporated in the constitutions and laws of many countries.

For the first time in history, the international community embraced a document considered to have universal value—"a common standard of achievement for all peoples and all nations". Its Preamble acknowledges the importance of a human rights legal framework to maintaining international peace and security, stating that recognition of the inherent dignity and equal and inalienable rights of all individuals is the foundation of freedom, justice and peace in the world. Elaborating the United Nations Charter's declared purpose of promoting social progress and well-being in larger freedom, the Declaration gives equal importance to economic, social and cultural rights and to civil rights and political liberties, and affords them the same degree of protection. The Declaration has inspired more than 60 international human rights instruments, which together constitute a comprehensive system of legally binding treaties for the promotion and protection of human rights.

Article 1

Right to Freedom and Equality in Dignity and Rights

The Universal Declaration covers the range of human rights in 30 clear and concise articles. The first two articles lay the universal foundation of human rights: human beings are equal because of their shared essence of human dignity; human rights are universal, not because of any State or international organisation, but because they belong to all of humanity. The two articles assure that human rights are the birth right of everyone, not privileges of a select few, nor privileges to be granted or denied. Article 1 declares that "all human beings are born equal in dignity and rights. They are endowed with reason and conscience and should act towards one another in a spirit of brotherhood." Article 2 recognises the universal dignity of a life free from discrimination. "Everyone is entitled to all the rights and freedoms set forth in this Declaration without distinction of any kind such as race, colour, sex, language, religion, political or other opinion, national or social origin, property, birth or other status."

The first cluster of articles, 3 to 21, sets forth civil and political rights to which everyone is entitled. The right to life, liberty and personal security, recognised in Article 3, sets the base for all following political rights and civil liberties, including freedom from slavery, torture and arbitrary arrest, as well as the rights to a fair trial, free speech and free movement and privacy.

The second cluster of articles, 22 to 27, sets forth the economic, social and cultural rights to which all human beings are entitled. The cornerstone of these rights is Article 22, acknowledging that, as a member of society, everyone has the right to social security and is therefore entitled to the realisation of the economic, social and cultural rights "indispensable" for his or her dignity and free and full personal development. Five articles elaborate the rights necessary for the enjoyment of the fundamental right to social security, including economic rights related to work, fair remuneration and leisure, social rights concerning an adequate standard of living for health, well-being and education, and the right to participate in the cultural life of the community.

The Third and final cluster of articles, 28 to 30, provides a larger protective framework in which all human rights are to be universally enjoyed. Article 28 recognises the right to a social and international order that enables the realisation of human rights and fundamental freedoms. Article 29 acknowledges that, along with rights, human beings also have obligations to the community which also enable them to develop their individual potential freely and fully. Article 30, finally protects the interpretation of the articles of the Declaration from any outside interference contrary to the purposes and principles of the United Nations. It explicitly states that no State, group or person can claim, on the basis of the Declaration, to have the right to engage in any activity or to perform any act aimed at the destruction of any of the rights and freedoms set forth in the Universal Declaration.

International Bill of Human Rights

Once the Universal Declaration of Human Rights was adopted, the Commission on Human Rights, the premier human rights intergovernmental body within the United Nations, set out to translate its principles into international treaties that protected specific rights. Given the unprecedented nature of the task, the General Assembly decided to draft two Covenants codifying the two sets of rights outlined in the Universal Declaration: Civil and Political Rights and Economic, Social and Cultural Rights. The Member States debated the individual provisions for two decades, seeking to give explicit endorsement to certain aspects of the universality of human rights only implicitly referred to in the Universal Declaration, such as the right of all peoples to self-determination, as well as reference to certain vulnerable groups. Such as indigenous people and minorities.

Consensus was reached in 1966, and the United Nations General Assembly adopted the International Covenant on Economic, Social and Cultural Rights and the International Covenant on Civil and Political Rights that year. The preambles and articles 1, 2, 3, and 5 are virtually identical in both International Covenants. Both preambles recognise that human rights derive from the inherent dignity of human beings. Article 1 of each Covenant affirms that all peoples have the right of self-determination and that by virtue of that right they are free to determine their political status and to pursue their economic, social and cultural development. Article 2, in both cases, reaffirms the principle of non-discrimination, echoing the Universal Declaration, while Article 3 stresses that States should ensure the equal right of men and women to the enjoyment of all human rights. Article 5 of both Covenants echoes the final provision of the Universal Declaration providing safeguards against the destruction or undue limitation of any human right or fundamental freedom. Two Optional Protocols elaborate certain provisions of the Covenant on Civil and Political Rights, one providing for complaints by individuals, the other advocating the abolition of the death penalty.

When they entered into force in 1976, the two International Covenants made many of the provisions of the Universal Declaration effectively binding for States that ratified them. These two International Covenants, together with the Universal Declaration and the Optional Protocols, comprise the International Bill of Human Rights.

Drafting the Universal Declaration

The preparatory Work for the Universal Declaration of Human Rights is a remarkable and early example of the Organization's capacity to bring about international cooperation and consensus. The text was drafted in two years—between January 1947, when the Commission on Human Rights first met to prepare an international Bill of Human Rights and December 1948, when the General Assembly adopted the Universal Declaration. An eight-member drafting committee prepared the preliminary text of the Universal Declaration. The Committee, chaired by Mrs. Eleanor Roosevelt, widow of the former United States President, agreed on the central importance of affirming universal respect for human rights and fundamental freedoms, including the principles of non-discrimination and civil and political rights, as well as social, cultural and economic rights. The Commission then revised the draft declaration, in the light of replies from Member States, before submitting it to the General Assembly.

The General Assembly, in turn, scrutinised the document, with the 58 Member States voting a total of 1,400 times on practically every word and every clause of the text. There were many debates. Some Islamic States objected to the articles on equal marriage rights and on the right to change religious belief, for example, while several Western countries criticised the inclusion of economic, social and cultural rights. On 10 December 1948, the United Nations General Assembly unanimously adopted the Universal Declaration of Human Rights, with 8 abstentions. Since then, 10 December is celebrated every year worldwide as Human Rights Day. The adoption of the Declaration was immediately hailed as a triumph, uniting very diverse and even conflicting political regimes, religious systems and cultural traditions. During 1998, the fiftieth anniversary of the Universal Declaration is being commemorated all over the world as Human Rights Year.

Article 2

Freedom from Discrimination

Over 60 human rights treaties elaborate fundamental rights and freedoms contained in the International Bill of Human Rights, addressing concerns such as slavery, genocide, humanitarian law, the administration of justice, social development, religious tolerance, cultural cooperation, discrimination, violence against women, and the status of refugees and minorities. The following four Conventions, relating to racial discrimination, torture, women and children, are considered core human rights treaties, together with the two International Covenants:

- The *International Convention on the Elimination of All Forms of Racial Discrimination* (adopted in 1965/ entry into force 1969) was a ground-breaking treaty defining and condemning racial discrimination. Calling for national measures towards the advancement of specific racial or ethnic groups, the Convention also makes the dissemination of ideas based on racial superiority or inspiring racial hatred punishable by law.

- The *Convention on the Elimination of All Forms of Discrimination against Women* (1979/1981) specifies measures for the advancement and empowerment of women in private and public life, particularly in the areas of education, employment, health marriages and the family.
- The *Convention against Torture and Other Cruel, Inhuman or Degrading Treatment or Punishment* (1984/1987) bans torture and rape as weapons of war. In 1998, in a major effort to help torture victims and to step up international attempts to end torture the United Nations declared 26 June as the annual International Day in Support of Victims of Torture.
- The *Convention on the Rights of the Child* (1989/1990) is the most universally ratified human rights Convention. Only two Member States, the United States and Somalia, are not yet parties to the Convention, which protects children, among other things, from economic and sexual exploitation.

Some 14 States have incorporated provisions of the Convention on the Rights of the Child into their constitutions, while 35 have passed new laws conforming to the Convention or amended laws related to child abuse, child labour and adoption. Other Member States have extended the length of compulsory education, guaranteed child refugees and minority children special protection or reformed juvenile justice systems, as stipulated by the Convention.

World Conference on Human Rights

The United Nations designated 1968 as the International Year for Human Rights to mark the twentieth anniversary of the Universal Declaration on Human Rights, and convened an International Conference on Human Rights in Tehran, Iran, to enhance national and international human rights efforts and initiatives. After evaluating the impact of the Universal Declaration on national legislation and judicial decisions, the Conference approved the Proclamation of Tehran, which formulated a programme for the future, addressing the problems of colonialism, racial discrimination, illiteracy and the protection of the family. The Tehran Proclamation emphasised particularly the principle of non-discrimination, condemning the policy of apartheid as a "crime against humanity", and urged the international community to ratify the International Covenants on Civil and Political Rights and on Economic, Social and Cultural Rights adopted by the United Nations two years earlier.

The World Conference on Human Rights in Vienna reassessed the progress of United Nations human rights work over the years. The Vienna Conference was marked by an unprecedented degree of support by the international human rights community. Some 7,000 participants, including delegations from 171 States and representatives of more than 840 non-governmental organisations gathered for two weeks to set out a revitalised programme for global human rights action. There was broad consensus that, with fundamental rights codified and the essential machinery in place, it was time to implement the established human rights standards and norms with greater vigilance.

In adopting the Vienna Declaration and Programme of Action by consensus, the World Conference reaffirmed the centrality of the Universal Declaration for human rights protection, and recognised, for the first time unanimously, the right to development as an inalienable right and an integral part of international human rights law. The Conference also emphasised that, as human rights are universal and indivisible as well as interrelated and interdependent, they should be promoted in equal manner. The delegates rejected arguments that some human rights were optional or subordinate to cultural traditions and practices. The Vienna Conference thus gave high priority to preserving the integrity of the Universal Declaration. Giving new impetus to the worldwide implementation of human rights norms, the Conference emphasised that most violations could be addressed by forcefully implementing existing norms through the mechanisms already available.

Article 3

Right to Life, Liberty and Security of Person

Stating that the protection and promotion of human rights are the "first responsibility" of Governments, the Vienna Declaration recognised democracy as a human right, thus strengthening the promotion of democracy and the rule of law. Also, giving high priority to the universal ratification of international human rights treaties, the World Conference urged States especially to ratify promptly the convention on the Rights of the Child and the Convention on the Elimination of All Forms of Discrimination against Women. Similarly, the Conference took innovative steps to protect the rights of vulnerable groups and to bring women's rights into the mainstream of United Nations human rights work, supporting the establishment of a Special Rapporteur on violence against women and calling for an international decade of the world's indigenous peoples.

The World Conference had a catalytic role in revitalizing the human rights programme of the United Nations. The Vienna Declaration and Programme of Action provides the international community with a new framework of planning, dialogue and cooperation that enables an integrated approach to promoting human rights. The recognition of the interdependence between democracy, development and human rights, for example, laid the groundwork for increased cooperation among international development agencies and national organisations in promoting human rights. The Vienna Declaration states, for the first time explicitly, that all organs, programmes and specialised agencies of the United Nations system should have a central role in strengthening human rights. Its key institutional recommendation, however, was the establishment of the post of United Nations High Commissioner for Human Rights to coordinate all human rights activities system-wide. The World Conference also called for a comprehensive five-year review of the progress made in the implementation of the Vienna Declaration and Programme of Action in 1998.

HUMAN RIGHTS IN ACTION

The United Nations has been adapting its human rights machinery in order to better respond to the changing demands of the international community. During the cold war, the United Nations created the normative and institutional structures for international human rights protection, steadily broadening its competence in this area. At the same time, it supported the vast process of decolonization, which led to the birth of over 80 new independent nations. Landmark United Nations actions, such as the Declaration on the Granting of Independence to Colonial Countries and Peoples (1960), provided the blueprint for universally establishing the collective right to self-determination. The United Nations also concentrated its efforts on the human rights abuses resulting from the policy of apartheid in South Africa, overseeing international action which eventually helped to end this gross abrogation of fundamental rights. Despite these successes, however, the effectiveness of the United Nations was severly restricted by the cold war, both in terms of the range of human rights to be defended and in terms of ensuring their respect in practice. The world political situation did not allow for much concerted human rights activism in the field. Doctrines of national security and sovereignty were often invoked to conceal, excuse or justify human rights abuses.

Today, there is widespread recognition that the 50-year investment in development and human rights promotion requires new impetus to secure broader realisation of economic and social rights. Extreme poverty and exclusion from economic, political and cultural life continue to be the fate of millions in both developing and developed countries. Currently, there are 48 countries where more than one fifth of the population live in "absolute poverty", with little prospect of dramatic change in the short term. Breaking the cycle of poverty thus continues to be a formidable task for the international community. For this reason, the United Nations has increasingly emphasised the right to development, which can provide the basis for a strategy for a more comprehensive human rights programme.

Strengthening the Human Rights Machinery

In the wake of the Vienna Conference, the United Nations has intensified efforts to refocus its human rights programme, shifting its main concern from standards setting to implementation. This effort was led by the main intergovernmental body in this area, the United Nations Commission on Human Rights, supported by the secretariat of the United Nations Centre for Human Rights. In 1993, the General Assembly significantly strengthened the Organisation's human rights machinery by creating the post of United Nations High Commissioner for Human Rights.

Mandated to coordinate all United Nations human rights programmes and improve their impact and overall efficiency, the High Commissioner is the chief official responsible for human rights. Operating under the direction and authority of the Secretary-General as his representative in the field of human rights, the High Commissioner also reports to the General Assembly, the Economic and Social Council and the Commission on Human Rights. The Office of the United Nations High Commissioner for Human Rights (OHCHR) serves as the secretariat of the Commission on Human Rights, the treaty bodies and other United Nations human rights organs, and is the focal point for all United Nations human rights activities.

The first High Commissioner was Mr. José Ayala Lasso, who served from 1994 to 1997. Having assumed office only one day before the outbreak of genocidal killing in Rwanda, Mr. Ayala Lasso called for the convening of an emergency session of the Commission on Human Rights to address the human rights situation in that country. The Rwandan tragedy made clear the need to strengthen the range of human rights instruments at the disposal of the United Nations.

In 1997, as part of wide-ranging reforms to enhance the effectiveness of the United Nations, Secretary-General Kofi Annan placed human rights at the heart of all the work of the Organisation, The Secretary-General organised the work of the United Nations into four substantive fields—peace and security, economic and social affairs, development cooperation, and humanitarian affairs—with human rights as the issue fifth priority area across each of these four programme fields. The United Nations is thus enhancing its human rights programme by integrating a human rights focus into the entire range of the Organization's activities. In addition, the High Commissioner's Office and the Centre for Human Rights were consolidated into a single Office of the United Nations High Commissioner for Human Rights. This merger gave the new High Commissioner a solid institutional basis from which to lead, as the focal point of all system-wide integration of human rights activities, the Organisation's mission in the domain of human rights.

Article 4

Freedom from Slavery and Servitude

Office of the United Nations High Commissioner for Human Rights

Ms. Mary Robinson, the former President of Ireland, assumed her post as the second High Commissioner for Human Rights in September 1997. The High Commissioner's mandate has four essential components:

- Building global partnerships for human rights;
- Preventing human rights violations and responding to emergencies;
- Promoting human rights, together with democracy and development, as the guiding principles for lasting peace; and
- Coordinating the system-wide strengthening of the United Nations human rights programme.

The Office of the High Commissioner, based in Geneva with country offices around the world, has a staff of some 200; its three main components deal with activities and programmes, research and right to development, and support services. The Office has a limited annual budget of about $20

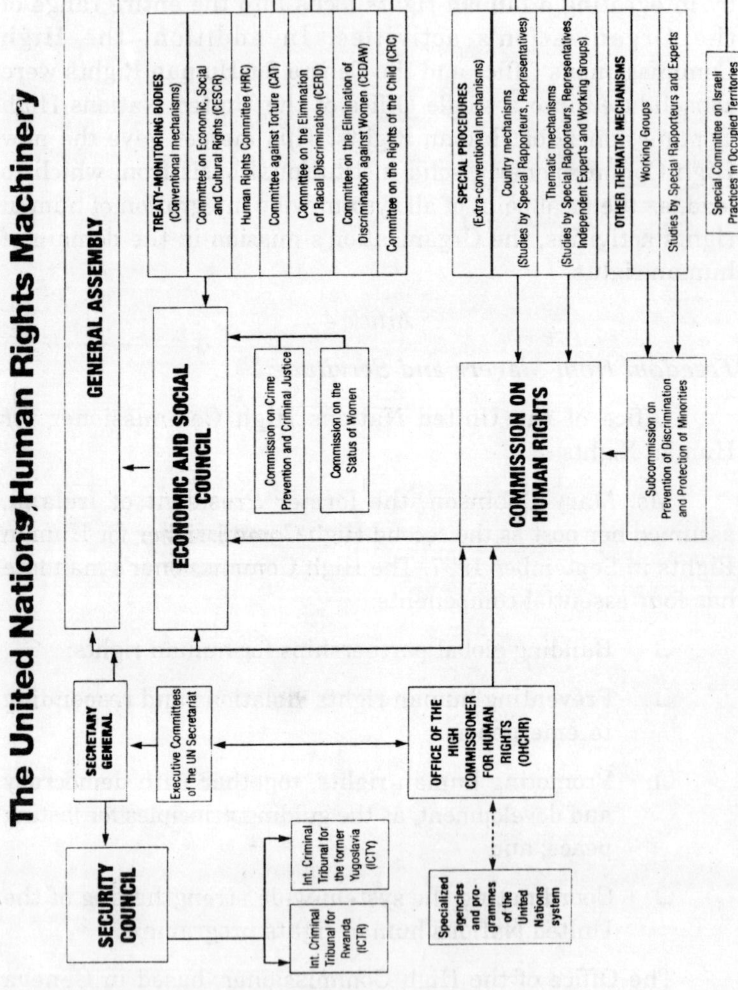

The United Nations Human Rights Machinery
GENERAL ASSEMBLY
TREATY-MONITORING BODIES (Conventional mechanisms)
Committee on Economic, Social and Cultural Rights (CESCR)
Human Rights Committee (HRC)
Committee against Torture (CAT)
Committee on the Elimination of Racial Discrimination (CERD)
Committee on the Elimination of Discrimination against Women (CEDAW)
Committee on the Rights of the Child (CRC)
SPECIAL PROCEDURES (Extra-conventional mechanisms)
Country mechanisms (Studies by Special Rapporteurs, Representatives)
Thematic mechanisms (Studies by Special Rapporteurs, Representatives, Independent Experts and Working Groups)
OTHER THEMATIC MECHANISMS
Working Groups
Studies by Special Rapporteurs and Experts
Special Committee on Israeli Practices in Occupied Territories
ECONOMIC AND SOCIAL COUNCIL
Commission on Crime Prevention and Criminal Justice
Commission on the Status of Women
COMMISSION ON HUMAN RIGHTS
Subcommission on Prevention of Discrimination and Protection of Minorities
SECRETARY GENERAL
Executive Committees of the UN Secretariat
OFFICE OF THE HIGH COMMISSIONER FOR HUMAN RIGHTS (OHCHR)
SECURITY COUNCIL
Int. Criminal Tribunal for the former Yugoslavia (ICTY)
Int. Criminal Tribunal for Rwanda (ICTR)
Specialized agencies and programmes of the United Nations system

million, about 1.7 per cent of the United Nations regular budget. However, the growing number of human rights activities in the field has led to a sharp increase in costs. Overall funding requirements for 1998 were $54 million. The High Commissioner's broadened mandate supports the work of the Commission on Human Rights and the treaty bodies, focusing, among other things, on advancing the rights of women and children, combating racial discrimination in all its forms and protecting vulnerable groups and minorities, such as indigenous people, migrants and disabled people.

In order to carry out these expanded mandates, the office increasingly relies on voluntary contributions to finance its activities. The Human Rights Field Operation in Rwanda, for example, was funded entirely by voluntary contributions from Governments. Several voluntary funds support the High Commissioner's initiatives on indigenous people, the rights of the child, economic rights, victims of torture and contemporary forms of slavery, as well as combating racism and racial discrimination.

Especially through the expansion of its technical cooperation programme, OHCHR has been able to provide human rights support to virtually all programmes and agencies within the United Nations system. In the area of peackeeping, for example, the programme has provided various forms of assistance to major United Nations missions in Angola, Cambodia, Mozambique, Haiti and the countries of the former Yugoslavia. It has also advised the United Nations electoral missions in Eritrea and South Africa. Such advisory services often entail the provision of human rights expertise, legislative analysis and training for personnel. The increased focus on joint operations has made it possible to fund a presence in the field through the regular budgets of the wider United Nations system.

Today, virtually every United Nations body and specialised agency, including the World Bank and the International Monetary Fund, is making efforts to incorporate the promotion or protection of human rights into its programmes and activities, including a gender perspective and an emphasis on the right to development OHCHR is taking other steps to strengthen the United Nations human rights machinery by supporting the human rights bodies and monitoring mechanisms in their efforts to streamline their work.

Commission on Human Rights

United Nations policy on human rights is governed, through the General Assembly, by a number of intergovernmental bodies, which also provide guidance to OHCHR. The main intergovernmental policy-making body concerned with human rights issues is the Commission on Human Rights. Established in 1946 by the Economic and Social Council, the Commission provides overall policy guidance, studies human rights problems, develops and codifies new international norms, and monitors the observance of human rights around the world. Made up of 53 Member States elected for three-year terms, the Commission provides a forum for States and intergovernmental and non-governmental organisations (NGOs) to voice their concerns about human rights issues.

Article 5

Freedom from Torture or Degrading Treatment

The Commission originally concentrated its efforts on defining and codifying international human rights standards. In the past two decades, however, the Commission has set up a system of special procedures to investigate alleged violations of human rights, and routinely dispatches fact finding missions to countries in all parts of the world. Today, the Commission's annual six-week session in Geneva provides a unique global forum for raising, discussing and clarifying allegations of a wide range of violations. States as well as NGOs present information on situations of concern to them; the Governments involved often submit replies. In the light of the examination of such situations, fact-finding groups of experts may be designated, on-the-spot visits may be organised discussions with

Governments pursued, assistance provided and violations condemned.

In recent years, the Commission has increasingly turned its attention to the promotion of economic, social and cultural rights, including the right to development. It has established a number of subsidiary bodies to assist its work in this area, such as the working groups on the effects of foreign-debt burdens and the impact of extreme poverty on the enjoyment of human rights.

High on the Commission's agenda are the promotion of women's rights and the protection of the rights of the child. Special attention is given to children in situations of armed conflict, to violence against women, including against women migrant workers, and to trafficking in women and girls. The Commission has further sought to protect the rights of vulnerable groups, particularly ethnic, religious and linguistic minorities and indigenous people. For this reason, it is seeking to create a permanent forum for indigenous people within the United Nations system.

Since 1948, the Commission has been assisted by the 26-member Subcommission on *Prevention of Discrimination and Protection of Minorities,* composed of independent experts from all regions of the world. The Subcommission, in turn, has established several working groups, which serve as forums for interaction between Governments and civil society concerning the rights of indigenous people, minorities and groups vulnerable to contemporary forms of slavery. Among other issues, the Subcommission focuses on contemporary forms of slavery, including forced labour, illegal and pseudo-legal adoptions aiming at the exploitation of children, and sexual slavery during wartime. It also considers human rights issues concerning domestic and migrant workers and examines preventive measures for the elimination of violence against women, in particular in situations of armed conflict.

Monitoring Human Rights Violations

An integral part of the body of human rights law provides for a monitoring role for the United Nations. At the heart of the United Nations monitoring system are two types of human rights mechanisms—conventional and extra-conventional—which respond to individual human rights abuses and to the systematic abrogation of rights by Member States.

Six core human rights treaties provide for so-called conventional monitoring mechanisms consisting of six treaty bodies or committees, which monitor States parties' adherence to the international standards established in the treaties. However, States parties must ratify these treaties before their principles and standards apply to them.

The *Human Rights Committee* monitors implementation of the International Covenant on Civil and Political Rights.

The *Committee on Economic, Social and Cultural Rights* monitors implementation of the International Covenant on Economic, Social and Cultural Rights.

The *Committee on the Elimination of Racial Discrimination* monitors implementation of the International Convention on the Elimination of All Forms of Racial Discrimination.

The *Committee on the Elimination of Discrimination against Women* monitors implementation of the Convention on the Elimination of All Forms of Discrimination against Women.

The *Committee against Torture* monitors implementation of the Convention against Torture and Other Cruel, Inhuman or Degrading Treatment or Punishment.

The *Committee on the Rights of the Child* monitors implementation of the Convention on the Rights of the Child.

In periodic reports to the committees, States parties outline the legislative, judical and administrative measures taken to ensure that government policies and practices conform to treaty principles. The Human Rights committee, for example, has considered over 800 reports with respect to 56 countries and published 270 decisions. While the committees' views are not legally binding, they possess significant weight.

States have frequently followed their decisions and made constitutional changes or adjusted their policies as a result of their recommendations.

Three human rights treaties allow for communications from individuals. The Human Rights Committee, the Committee against Torture and the Committee on the Elimination of Racial Discrimination are authorised to accept individual complaints from citizens of States that have ratified the respective provisions concerning individual communications. Two specialised agencies, the United Nations Educational, Scientific and Cultural Organisation (UNESCO) and the International Labour Organisation (ILO), also examine alleged discrimination in their respective fields of competence.

In 1967, the Economic and Social Council adopted resolution 1235 (XLII), authorising the Commission on Human Rights and its Subcommission on Prevention of Discrimination and Protection of Minorities to examine information relevant to gross violations of human rights and fundamental freedoms. In 1970, the Council adopted resolution 1503 (XLVIII), establishing a mechanism to respond to complaints by individuals, now commonly known as the "1503 procedure". The allegations are summarised in confidential documents sent to the Commission on Human Rights for review. If a consistent pattern of verified and serious human rights abuse is evident, the Commission can investigate the situation through its system of "special procedures".

The Office of the High Commissioner for Human Rights maintains a 24-hour fax "hot line" (0041-22-917-0092) for reporting alleged human rights violations. Each year, it receives nearly 200,000 communications reporting violations.

Article 6

Right to Recognition as a Person Before the Law

Special Procedures

The United Nations human rights programme relies increasingly on an independent system of fact-finding outside the treaty framework, which permits a more flexible approach to individual violations. This system of so-called extra-conventional mechanisms refers to the special procedures of the Commission on Human Rights. The Commission can appoint independent experts of international stature to examine, monitor and publicly report either on the situation of human rights in specific countries or, in the case of a thematic mandate, on serious human rights violations related to certain phenomena in various parts of the world, such as religious intolerance or the use of mercenaries. These experts, acting in their personal capacity, are designated as special rapporteurs, representatives, independent experts or, when several experts share a mandate, working groups.

The special rapporteurs are free to use all reliable sources available to them to prepare their reports, and much of their research is done in the field, where they conduct interviews with authorities, NGOs and victims, gathering on-site evidence whenever possible. In 1997, there were fact-finding missions to 14 countries; and inquiries regarding more than 5,000 cases were transmitted to Governments. The special rapporteurs report annually to the Commission on Human Rights, with recommendations for action. Their findings are also used by the treaty bodies in their work, especially in evaluating States' reports.

As of mid-1998, there were over 20 country mandates on the human rights situation in specific regions. Country rapporteurs generally monitor the complex human rights situation in regions where massive violations have occurred, often in the aftermath of large-scale violence or conflict, as in Cambodia, Rwanda and the Former Yugoslavia. They make recommendations on how human rights can be strengthened at the national level. The Commission on Human Rights appointed a Special Rapporteur on the human rights situation in Rwanda in May 1994, while the genocide was still ongoing, to examine all human rights aspects of the situation, including root causes and responsibilities for the atrocities. In 1997, the Commission followed up on that three-year mandate by appointing a Special Representative to facilitate the creation and effective functioning of an independent national human rights commission in Rwanda.

The General Assembly also requested the Secretary-General to investigate the systematic rape and abuse of women and children during the armed conflict in the former Yugoslavia, Particularly in the Republic of Bosnia and Herzegovina.

The experts entrusted with thematic mandates cover a range of specific human rights issues of worldwide significance. The right to life, for instance, is recognised as the most fundamental right, and its violation by States is an issue of international concern. The Working Group on Enforced and Involuntary Disappearances established in 1980, was the first to take up individual complaints and visit States. In 1995, one of the experts of the Working Group began to examine the problem of missing persons in the former Yugoslavia. In his final report of 1997, the expert reported that in Bosnia and Herzegovina, some 20,000 persons were still missing, the great majority of whom—Bosnian men of Muslim origin—were victims of systematic "ethnic cleansing" operations carried out by Bosnian Serb forces between 1992 and 1995.

In 1997, the Special Rapporteur on violence against women visited Rwanda to study the issue of violence against women in wartime and in post-conflict situations and met with numerous women survivors. The Special Rapporteur also visited the International Criminal Tribunal for Rwanda in Tanzania, where she observed the trial of Jean-Paul Akayesu—the first such trial which included charges of sexual violence in the indictment.

Since 1982, the Special Rapporteur on extrajudicial, summary on arbitrary executions has been entrusted with the investigation of violations of the right to life committed by State authorities or armed groups. Working closely with Governments, United Nations bodies and NGOs, the Special Rapporteur appeals to Governments to prevent executions, particularly when the right to a fair trial seems to have been violated. The Rapporteur responds to information on death threats against individuals and deaths in custody, calling for public inquiries or submitting urgent appeals.

Emergency Measures

Special rapporteurs sometimes submit urgent appeals to Governments if they learn of serious human rights violations about to be committed against individuals or vulnerable groups, such as refugees or indigenous communities. In 1997, close to 400 urgent interventions were made to prevent possible violations, particularly in cases of threatened or actual disappearances, possible torture and imminent executions. In 1995, the Special Rapporteur on torture sent 68 letters to 61 Governments regarding 669 cases, as well as 130 urgent appeals on behalf of nearly 500 people. Some 42 countries responded in 459 of those cases. Between 1992 and 1996, the Special Rapporteur on extrajudicial, summary or arbitrary executions made 818 urgent appeals on behalf of more than 6,500 persons to 91 different countries and received replies in roughly half of the instances. In his 1997 report, the Special Rapporteur noted that violations of the rights to life were still on the rise. That year, the Special Rapporteur acted on more than 960 cases of alleged violations of the right to life, submitting 122 urgent appeals on behalf of 3,720 persons.

Civil Society—Partners in Human Rights Action

The United Nations believes that creating a pervasive culture of human rights requires a dynamic network of partnerships worldwide. The High Commissioner for Human Rights implements her broad mandate in partnership with a variety of actors, including the programmes and agencies within the United Nations system, Governments, regional organisations, academic communities, committed individuals and the NGO community. New types of partnerships are being developed with civil society. In the field of child rights, NGOs have participated in discussions relating to the preparation of government reports. With the help of the United Nations Children's Fund (UNICEF) they have submitted their own information to the Committee on the Rights of the Child, attended the Committee's sessions and monitored, at the national level, the implementation of its recommendations.

NGOs and other representatives of civil society, such as academic institutions and citizens' groups, have been crucial to the United Nations human rights work since its inception—from the inclusion of human rights clauses in the Charter to the establishment of the Office of the High Commissioner for Human rights. NGOs have also been key to developing human rights priorities in the major world conferences of this decade—particularly the agreements achieved on human rights in Vienna (1993), on population and development in Cairo (1994), on social development in Copenhagen (1995), on women's rights in Beijing (1995) and on food security in Rome (1996).

NGOs provide leadership in other areas too. In the preparation of the Rome Conference which approved the establishment of an International Criminal Court in July 1998, a well-informed and vocal NGO coalition was instrumental in pushing for a strong mandate for the Court. The Coalition often led the debate on contentious issues such as the need for an independent prosecutor and the inclusion of the crime of aggression as one of the core crimes under the Court's jurisdiction. The strong NGO partnership with Governments and the United Nations ensured that the International Criminal Court, the last international institution expected to be created in this century, possesses the capacity to exercise its dual purpose of prosecuting individuals responsible for atrocities and deterring future barbarities.

The strength of non-governmental human rights organisations lies in their ability to mobilize public opinion, disseminate information and pressure Governments to conform to international human rights standards. There is great diversity among these NGOs. Some defend all human rights in general, while others protect the specific rights of particular vulnerable groups, such as women and children, or deal with urgent human rights issues, such as torture, enforced disappearances or the treatment of prisoners.

Article 7

Right to Equal Consideration Before the Law

NGOs are vital actors in human rights advocacy: representing and protecting victims, providing expertise, collecting and disseminating information and encouraging human rights education. Among human rights NGOs, women's groups are among the most active in the world today, playing a vital role in the advancement and empowerment of women by increasing awareness of women's issues, as well as educating women in their human rights. Many other NGOs have an indirect role in defending human rights. They focus primarily on other issues but have incorporated human rights into their activities and, by offering legal assistance to vulnerable groups, advance the cause of human rights.

Some human rights organisations, such as Human Rights Watch and the International Federation for Human Rights, have a large international reach, and conduct independent surveys, publish newsletters and disseminate detailed reports. Today, there are hundreds of NGOs whose human rights work has taken on a transnational character. Amnesty International, for example, the largest human rights NGO, with 1.2 million members in 160 countries, recently launched a worldwide petition drive to secure the commitment of over 6 million people to the Universal Declaration of Human Rights. The pledges will be handed over to the United Nations General Assembly on Human Rights Day, 10 December, on the occasion of the fiftieth anniversary of the Universal Declaration.

Defending Human Rights Defenders

Around the world, there is a small but vital community of human rights defenders, comprising representatives of NGOs and other individuals or associations, all involved in the "front-line" struggle for human rights. Some are non-governmental organisation volunteers, lawyers or journalists; others are peasant leaders, students or relatives of victims. Often they are part of local organisations, which do not benefit from the protection of a large international association and are vulnerable to attacks. Their work is especially important in countries recovering from armed conflict, suffering the consequences of dictatorship or undergoing major social and political transformations.

Watching that Governments live up to their promises and obligations to protect and promote the rights of their citizens, human rights defenders are often at considerable risk of becoming themselves victims of serious violations, facing death threats, arrest and detention or suffering abduction and torture. Many have lost their lives while defending human rights.

In 1985, to protect human rights activists and NGOs, the Commission on Human Rights established a working group to draft a declaration aimed at guaranteeing individuals the right to publicly denounce violations, to form and participate in human rights NGOs and to communicate with international human rights organisations. In 1998, after more than 13 years of discussion, the Commission adopted the draft Declaration on the Right and Responsibility of Individuals, Groups and Organs of Society to Promote and Protect Universally Recognised Human Rights and Fundamental Freedoms, also known as the Declaration on Human Rights Defenders. The Declaration is not a legally binding treaty. But clarifies and reinforces rights that are already recognised in existing international instruments.

A COMPREHENSIVE APPROACH TO HUMAN RIGHTS

The international human rights standards and norms adopted through the United Nations represent the hard-won consensus of the international community, not the hegemony of any particular region or set of traditions. The international human rights instruments establish minimum standards for the range of economic, social, cultural, civil and political rights. But they do not impose a single cultural standard; rather, they promote a common legal standard of respect for human dignity. Within this international framework, States have sovereign power to adapt human rights to their national settings, as long as they do not contradict the norms established through international human rights treaties.

A fundamental tenet of international human rights law is that all human rights are of equal importance. In practical terms, this means that they must be viewed collectively and that a comprehensive and balanced approach in promoting these rights must be found. No set of rights—say, cultural rights —can be given pre-eminence over other human rights without distorting the principles of indivisibility and interdependence. Every human being, for example, has the right to participate in the cultural life of his or her community. The right to practise one's cultural belief, however, is limited at the point at which it infringes on another human right. This means that cultural rights cannot be invoked or interpreted in such a way as to justify any act leading to the denial or violation of other human rights and fundamental freedoms.

Despite its commitment to protect all human rights, the United Nations in reality has promoted civil and political rights much more than economic, social and cultural rights in the past decades. This imbalance is reflected in the Universal Declaration itself. Eighteen articles deal in great detail with civil and political rights, while only six articles deal with economic, social and cultural rights. Since 1993, guided by the Vienna Declaration and Programme of Action, the United Nations has been addressing this imbalance by giving economic, social and cultural rights the same priority as civil and political rights within a human rights framework based on a unifying set of standards. The Organisation also emphasises the right to development as a human right, for it offers an integrated approach to all human rights, an approach which promises to overcome this artificial split between two sets of rights, thus allowing for a cohesive strategy to strengthen human rights.

Civil and Political Rights

The United Nations protect the civil and political rights of individuals and groups through a number of international treaties, but particularly through the International Covenant on Civil and Political Rights. The Covenant deals with such rights as freedom of movement; equality before the law; the right to a fair trial and presumption of innocence; freedom of thought, conscience and religion and religion; freedom of opinion and expression; freedom of association, participation in public affairs and elections; and protection of minority rights.

The Human Rights Committee plays a central role in monitoring its implementation, clarifying contentious issues concerning individual rights. Indeed, civil and political rights, including those concerning free speech, assembly and religion, have become to entrenched in international human rights law that States can no longer claim to violate them unknowingly. However, the need for protection has not diminished. Even though states of emergency can no longer be inconsistent with obligations under international law, Government frequently use national security concerns as a pretext for infringing on civil and political rights, especially in their treatment of dissident groups and critical members of the press.

Serious violations of the fundamental right to life, liberty and personal security have not abated. Hundreds of persons disappear every year or are the victims of torture or extrajudicial killings. The United Nations investigates gross human rights violations through the working groups on arbitrary detention and enforced or involuntary disappearances, as well as the special rapporteurs on extra judical, summary or arbitrary executions and on torture.

The Special Rapporteur on torture, for example, plays a key role in the international fight against cruel and inhuman punishment by responding to complaints from individuals and groups. In 1981, the United Nations set up a Voluntary Fund for Victims of Torture. Since its inception, the Fund has financed over 300 projects, giving priority to those providing direct medical or psychological assistance to torture victims. The United Nations also urges all States to provide for compensation and rehabilitation of torture victims in their domestic law.

Economic, Social and Cultural Rights

With the success of decolonisation and the increase in the number of newly independent States, the membership of the United Nations underwent a significant change. By the 1970s, developing countries represented a majority in the General Assembly, and their concerns and priorities became increasingly reflected in the work of the General Assembly—particularly the issue of economic and social development. Reflecting this overall change of emphasis the main thrust of United Nations work in the area of human rights today has been to strengthen the promotion of economic, social and cultural rights, particularly the right to development.

The United Nations has provided leadership in articulating the inherent relationship between human rights and economic and social development, providing a framework in which they reinforce each other. Beginning in the 1970s, the Commission on Human Rights turned its attention to the obstacles hindering the full realisation of economic, social and cultural rights, particularly in developing countries. The landmark achievement of the Commission was the drafting of the Declaration on the Right to Development, adopted by the General Assembly in 1986. It was the first time that the international community explicitly recognised the right to development as an inalienable and fundamental human right.

Article 8

Right to Remedy Through a Competent Tribunal

The Committee on Economic, Social and Cultural Rights has increasingly concentrated its efforts in establishing benchmarks for economic and social rights so that these rights can be more effectively implemented and monitored. At the national level, the strengthening of economic, social and cultural rights is being achieved through the provision of basic social services to all sectors of society; in agrarian economies, this is achieved by giving clear legal rights of ownership of land. But also crucial is the effective functioning of a free and fair legal system, protecting civil and political rights, such as freedom of expression, eliminating discrimination and, in particular, advancing the human rights of women. Benchmarks are crucial to improving accountability and to ensuring the standards and norms regarding economic, social and cultural rights are progressively raised to the same level as civil and political rights.

In recent years, a great deal of effort has been devoted to further elaborating the rights to adequate food, health care, housing and primary education. The right to food, for example, was affirmed by 186 countries at the 1996 World Food Summit. The right to adequate housing was the focus of the 1996 Habitat Conference in Istanbul. The United Nations estimates that 100 million people are homeless and 1 billion people inadequately housed worldwide. Due to the recommendations of the Committee on Economic, Social and Cultural Rights, several Governments have agreed to stop forced evictions and are now focusing on ways to guarantee housing. The Dominican Republic, after being criticised for inadequate housing, invited the Committee to carry out a survey mission and meet with non-governmental organisations. The Government of the Philippines recently reported to the Committee that it would increase its spending on new housing and had developed programmes to relocate and shelter homeless persons who had been evicted. Advancing the universal recognition of the right to education, the Committee recently persuaded Zimbabwe to abandon the charging of fees for primary education, a policy incompatible with the promotion of education as a human right.

The Right to Development

The right to development is the result of a conceptual evolution within the United Nations, shaped first by the experience of decolonisation and later by the recognition that developing countries need sustained assistance in order to create the conditions necessary for the universal enjoyment of human rights. The emphasis on the right to development reflects the conviction that a narrowly defined notion of economic development is not enough to create these conditions. Development that occurs without respect for human rights and the rule of the law remains incomplete. Development leads to the strengthening of human rights to the same degree that the promotion and protection of human rights provide the basis for sustainable development. In 1997, Secretary-General Kofi Annan stressed the crucial importance of the right to development for the international community.

"Truly sustainable development is possible only when the political, economic and social rights of all people are fully respected. They help to create the social equilibrium which is vital if a society is to evolve in peace. The right to development is the measure of respect of all other human rights. That should be our aim: a situation in which all individuals are enabled to maximise their potential, and to contribute to the evolution of society as a whole."

The universal right of peoples to self-determination in all its dimensions lies at the heart of the right to development. The 1986 Declaration on the Right to Development sees development as a complex, comprehensive and dynamic process, involving cultural, economic, political and social aspects, by which the well-being of all individuals and society as a whole is steadily improved. The aspects, by which the well-being of all individuals and society as a whole is steadily improved. The individual is recognised as the central subject of development, with rights as well as responsibilities regarding his or her participation in development. States have "primary responsibility" for creating the conditions enabling the realisation of the right to development, as both an individual and a collective right.

Participation is given special emphasis in the right to development, entailing the active, free and meaningful participation of individuals in the process and in the fair distribution of the resulting social benefits. The Declaration also provides for an international dimension in its implementation: developed countries should assist developing countries in creating the necessary conditions for development by reducing the negative aspects of international terms of trade, of foreign-debt repayments and of structural adjustment programmes.

The right to development has the potential to provide the integration of human rights that the international community has been striving to achieve for over five decades. This right not only encompasses all civil, cultural, economic, political and social rights, but it also promotes the recognition of interdependent and indivisible ties between various human rights, permitting the individual's full participation and involvement in economically durable, politically free and socially just development. These are long-term goals that have yet to be realised and will require the commitment and efforts of all development actors—from local and regional NGOs and national Governments to international organisations and global financial institutions.

In today's age of globalisation, where national economies become more and more interdependent, the United Nations recognises the need for closer partnerships with the private sector. There is a growing awareness that many decisions originating in the private sector have a direct or indirect impact on the global respect for human rights. Constructive cooperation between the United Nations and the business community is crucial in meeting the pressing challenge of implementing the right to development, promoting good governance and improving health and education.

Right to Development: Eradicating Poverty

Poverty is a condition that reflects the disregard for a wide range of human rights. Accordingly, the eradication of poverty remains one of the most important goals for United Nations activities in development and is a central theme of the right to development. A quarter of the population in the developing world lives in extreme poverty, while in many parts of the developed world the percentage of those living in poverty is increasing. Poverty affects a society in many ways. Since 70 per cent of the 1.6 billion people living in extreme poverty worldwide are women, United Nations efforts to eradicate poverty increasingly give special consideration to its female dimension. Women work two thirds of the world's working hours but earn only one tenth of the world's income and own less than one tenth of the world's property. In addition, two thirds of the world's illiterate are women. A women's right to development still encounters many barriers, rooted in domestic laws, cultural traditions, social practices and gender-based stereotypes that are extremely difficult to eradicate.

A rights-based approach to development provides the ethical foundation for concerted action against poverty and empowers the poor in their struggle for social justice. The United Nations helps Governments set targets and measure progress poverty reduction. Crucial to the success of these initiatives is the close involvement of NGOs representing the poor, and at the local level, the people themselves, in planning, implementing and evaluating development projects. Key to eradicating poverty is the sustained cooperation between developed and developing countries. One of the most promising recent initiatives, embraced by several United Nations agencies and funds, is the 20/20 Compact, which calls for developed and developing countries to allocate, on average, 20 per cent of official development assistance (ODA) and 20 per cent of national budgets to basic social programmes. In 1995, the World Summit for Social Development in Copenhagen and the World Conference on Women in Beijing endorsed the 20/20 Compact, recognizing that one of the most effective and efficient methods for poverty alleviation is the universal provision of basic social services.

Article 9

Freedom from Arbitrary Arrest or Exile

A milestone in this direction was the establishment of the United Nations Foundation in 1998, as a result of United States businessman Ted Turner's commitment to support the Organisation with $1 billion over a 10-year period. Also, Rotary Clubs worldwide have donated more than $400 million to the World Health Organisation (WHO). Major airlines have been working together with UNICEF by collecting over $ 18 million from passengers' donations of spare change in foreign currency. An Italian fashion group has lunched a global campaign promoting the fiftieth anniversary of the Universal Declaration of Human Rights. International banks are contributing to the United Nations Development Programme's programme of offering micro-credits to poor people to start their own business and create sustainable livelihoods.

Realizing the Right to Development

The 1993 World Conference on Human Rights dealt extensively with the right to development, linking it inextricably with democracy and peace. It recommended that the High Commissioner for Human Rights be given a specific mandate to promote the right to development, as well as to coordinate support from relevant bodies of the United Nations system for that purpose, Currently, the High Commissioner is reorienting the human rights programme to improve the implementation of economic, social and cultural rights by giving special attention to the right to development.

The agencies and programmes of the United Nations system are also incorporating the right to development into their activities, on the basis of a comprehensive rights-based approach to development. A rights-based approach not only defines beneficiaries according to their needs, but also recognises that the individuals receiving assistance are autonomous subjects with legitimate claims to the right to development. This rights-based framework introduces an important element of accountability, which promises to improve effectiveness and transparency of action.

Article 10

Right to a Fair Trial or Public Hearing

In response to the Secretary-General's reform efforts to integrate human rights into all aspects of the Organisation's work, the United Nations Development Programme (UNDP) issued in 1998 a policy document. "Integrating human rights with sustainable human development", which outlines the

UNDP's rights-based approach to development. The document takes the realisation of the right to development as its starting point. It deals with the human rights implications for sustainable human development and the effectiveness of UNDP support for human rights, and indicates ways of implementing the strategy including working closely with the Office of the High Commissioner for Human Rights. UNDP's human rights commitment provides a promising model for system-wide cooperation in human rights.

The promotion and protection of labour rights have been a central mandate of the International Labour Organisation (ILO) since its establishment in 1919. ILO, through its unique tripartite structure of government, business and labour representatives, formulates international policies and programmes to promote basic human rights, improve working conditions and expand employment. ILO develops and monitors labour standards in the workplace, through conventions and guidelines that have been incorporated in the national legislation of virtually all countries.

Other members of the United Nations system have also taken measures to advance human rights. The United Nations Children's Fund (UNICEF) uses the Convention on the Rights of the Child as a basis for dialogue with Governments. UNICEF strongly supports the work of the Committee on the Rights of the Child and other child rights initiatives. Promoting and protecting the right to food have led to cooperation between the Office of the High Commissioner and the Food and Agriculture Organisation of the United Nations (FAO). Similarly, the High Commissioner is developing close contacts with the United Nations Conference on Trade and Development (UNCTAD) and the United Nations Population Fund (UNFPA) to share expertise in areas relating to economic development and human rights.

STRENGTHENING HUMAN RIGHTS AT THE NATIONAL LEVEL

In recent years, the United Nations has concentrated its efforts on strengthening the promotion and protection of human rights at the national and local levels. There is a strong rationale for this. Human Rights are best secured when they have taken root in the local culture. International human rights standards can only be effective when they have been incorporated into national legislation and are promoted through national institutions. Still, many obstacles continue to impede the universal enjoyment of human rights at the national level. A number of Member States do not have adequate infrastructure to promote and protect their citizens' rights effectively. This is especially the case when they have recently emerged from bloody civil conflicts, as in Burundi, Cambodia, Rwanda, Sierra Leone and the former Yogoslavia.

There is another important reason for encouraging capacities at the national level. In the absence of sufficient resources, the United Nations human rights programme cannot routinely carry out comprehensive human rights field operations at the national level. The United Nations has therefore intensified its advisory services to Governments and greatly expanded its technical cooperation programmes within the larger framework of promoting democracy, development and human rights, strengthening the capacity of States to promote and protect human rights within their jurisdictions.

Technical Cooperation for Human Rights

The number of United Nations technical cooperation programmes in the field of human rights has risen from two projects in 1984 to nearly 200 annually now. The programmes, supervised by the Office of the High Commissioner for Human Rights (OHCHR), focus on countries in transition to democracy and on developing countries which request technical expertise in establishing national human rights structures. Human rights monitoring often takes place in conjunction with advisory services, complementing the technical assistance projects by identifying problems and providing feedback on their effectiveness.

The Human Rights Technical Cooperation Programme is financed from the regular budget of the United Nations and through the Voluntary Fund for Technical Cooperation in the

Field of Human Rights. Established in 1987, the Fund has received more than $19 million in voluntary contributions and pledges. The budgetary resources of the Technical Cooperation Programme for 1998 and 1999 total nearly $3.4 million. The allocations by region are Africa 31 per cent, Latin America and the Caribbean 20 per cent, Asia and the Pacific 18 per cent and Europe 9 per cent. Besides country-specific projects requested by States, OHCHR also undertakes technical cooperation projects with a global or thematic emphasis. Twenty per cent of the funds for technical cooperation are devoted to global projects, such as human rights education and training initiatives for the military and for peacekeeping operations. During 1997, a total to 43 technical cooperation projects were carried out of which 25 were at the national level, 9 at the regional level and 9 at the international level. By the beginning of 1998, there were ongoing projects in 58 countries.

OHCHR provides guidance in drafting legislative reforms that affect, directly or indirectly, the realisation of human rights. Legislation includes penal codes and prison regulations, codes of criminal procedure, laws affecting freedom of expression, association and assembly, immigration and nationality laws, minority protection, the judiciary and legal practice, and security legislation. The cooperation programme provides comprehensive technical assistance in the incorporation of international human rights standards and norms into national laws and policies, and helps in the establishment of national institutions capable of protecting human rights and promoting democracy and the rule of law.

OHCHR also helps Governments identify human rights issues and define policies, particularly through the formulation and implementation of comprehensive national plans of action. These plans, which can be relatively simple or prepared in great detail, identify national priorities in the promotion and protection of human rights and set targets and benchmarks, and often involve a wide range of human rights actors from both governmental institutions and civil society.

Article 11

Right to be Considered Innocent Until Proven guilty

Electoral Assistance

Various parts of the United Nations system provide assistance in the preparation and holding of elections. The Electoral Assistance Division of the United Nations Department of Political Affairs is the main Secretariat body assisting States in holding free and fair elections it has provided various forms of electoral assistance to over 80 countries, ranging from advisory services to election verification. The United Nations Development Programme (UNDP) provides technical support to electoral processes, helps countries to build electoral bodies and coordinates electoral assistance at election time. Since 1990, the technical cooperation programmes now under the coordination of OHCHR have provided electoral assistance by training electoral officials, preparing guidelines for electoral laws and procedures, publishing a handbook on human rights and elections and carrying out public information activities relating to human rights and elections. Countries that have received technical electoral assistance from OHCHR include Albania (1991), Angola (1992), Cambodia (1992), Eritrea (1992), Lesotho (1991-1993), Malawi (1992-1993), Romania (1990-1992) and South Africa (1993).

Human Rights and the Administration of Justice

Technical cooperation is vital in building and strengthening national infrastructures that have a direct impact on the rule of law and the overall respect for human rights. Such infrastructure work proceeds slowly, particularly where war or military rule has undermined the administration of justice. Crucial to rebuilding institutions of governance is an effective system of justice, as due process is almost always a casualty of military dictatorships and armed conflicts. In situations where the police and armed forces inspire fear and suspicion citizens cease to rely on them for protection. For this reason, OHCHR provides training in the administration of justice and law enforcement, so that lawmakers and law enforcement officers develop and enhance their role as human rights defenders.

Training courses for judges, lawyers, prosecutors, police officers and prison personnel aim at developing effective techniques for the ethical performance of penal and judical functions and law enforcement in a democratic society. Areas covered in these human rights courses include the independence of judges and lawyers, elements of a fair trial, juvenile justice, special protection of the rights of women and human rights under states of emergency. Law enforcement courses cover principles of ethical police conduct in democracies, the use of force in law enforcement, the human rights of suspects during criminal investigations, arrest and pre-trial detention, effective methods of ethical interrogation and the legal status and rights of the accused. Prison officials are instructed in the minimum standards for prisons and detention camps, in prison health issues, including AIDS/HIV, and in the treatment of special categories of delinquents, such as juveniles and women. Military personnel are trained in the principles of human rights and humanitarian law guiding their legitimate functions in society.

National Human Rights Institutions

The establishment and strengthening of national human rights institutions is perhaps the single most important component in the United Nations Technical Cooperation Programme. National human rights institutions are the primary mechanisms for translating international concepts and norms into a local culture of human rights. Two valuable bodies for human rights protection are the ombudsman, who serves as a focal point for complaints by individuals, and truth and reconciliation commissions, which are able to monitor the work of Governments from within and assist them in carrying out their treaty obligations under the human rights conventions. Their main functions are:

- ❑ Providing human rights expertise to Governments and parliaments;

- Investigating individual human rights violations;
- Conducting public inquiries into systematic or structural violations;
- Fostering human rights education.

Because these institutions are rooted in their local cultures, they can protect vulnerable groups and uphold international human rights standards without seeming alien to the national consensus. They can provide effective protection in a more informed manner and with greater attention to local cultural sensitivities than international or even regional organisations possibly could.

While most national human rights institutions can propose necessary legislative reforms or suggest changes in government policy, some ombudsmen also have the authority to conduct public inquiries on their own initiative to bring systematic and structural violations against vulnerable groups to public attention. One of the more important functions of a national human rights institution is, in fact, a side effect of its investigatory powers. As seen with the Truth and Reconciliation Commission in South Africa, the existence of a national mechanism with the power to investigate abuses and to provide compensation to victims may in itself, figure as a deterrent to future abuse. Another important role a national institution can perform is fostering human rights education with a strategic focus on preventive strategies.

Since the new emphasis on national institutions, beginning in 1995, the United Nations has been assisting an increasing number of States in establishing such institutions. During 1997, 18 States received advice or assistance: Armenia, Bangladesh, Cambodia, Fiji, Georgia, Liberia, Malawi, Madagascar, Mauritius, Mongolia, Nepal, Papua New Guinea, Rwanda, South Africa, Sri Lanka, Thailand, Uganda and Zambia. OHCHR has begun to work closely with UNDP to implement joint projects on national institutions, such as the recently established human rights institution for southern Africa.

The United Nations also assists in developing human rights structures at the regional level. It supported the first Regional Conference of African National Human Rights Institutions, held in 1996. Other regional forums that have received assistance are the African Commission on Human and Peoples' Rights, the African Centre for Democracy and Human Rights Studies in the Gambia and the Arab Institute for Human Rights in Tunis. There are now regional associations or periodic meetings of national institutions in Africa, the Asian-Pacific region. Latin America and Europe. In 1997, the national institutions in the Asian-Pacific region met in New Delhi and the Fourth International Workshop of National Institutions was held in Mexico.

Human Rights in Rwanda

For four years (1994-1998), the Human Rights Field Operation in Rwanda (HRFOR) provided technical assistance and monitored the critical human rights situation in that country. Financed entirely through voluntary contributions, HRFOR was the first human rights field operation to be run under the authority of the High Commissioner for Human Rights. At its peak, the operation had over 137 international staff members deployed in the country, with 58 observers still in Rwanda when it was shut down at the end of July 1998.

Human Rights in the Field

As human rights fieldwork is a relatively new area, it is still being shaped by the different needs of the individual countries and the experiences specific to each project. Some field operations derive from Security Council resolutions, as in the former Yugoslavia; others are authorised by the Commission on Human Rights or are the result of agreements between the High Commissioner and the country concerned. Some field offices are set up in cooperation with other multilateral institutions, such as the Organisation for Security and Cooperation in Europe, or directly established by the Office of the High Commissioner for Human Rights. In all cases, the field offices are supervised by the High Commissioner's Office and cooperate closely with other United Nations agencies and programmes. Today, human rights field activities are being carried out in 22 countries staffed by over 200 individuals, a significant increase in the programme, which began with one presence in 1992.

Human rights field offices often combine technical assistance with a monitoring function, such as gathering information, analysing the general human rights situation or reporting violations. In certain instances, these monitoring and protection activities in the field help create the conditions for ensuring the safe return of refugees or displaced persons in the aftermath of conflicts. Some field offices, such as those in Gaza, Malawi, Mongolia and South Africa, assist in development programmes building national capacity in the areas of legislation, the administration of justice and education. The field office for Gaza and the West Bank forms an integral part of a concerted international effort aimed at advancing the peace process and furthering the social and economic development of Palestine. The fieldwork in Gaza is based on a multidimensional strategy that focuses on establishing a legal framework consistent with human rights standards, developing a plan of action for an official human rights policy and strengthening structures to protect and promote human rights.

Human rights field operation priorities are clearly oriented towards technical cooperation, but monitoring continues to be necessary in order to assist Governments in introducing corrective measures when necessary. Monitoring is also useful in indentifying human rights initiatives that can be implemented by non-governmental institutions. The Human Rights Field Operation in the Former Yugoslavia (HRFOFY), for example, assists in the establishment of multi-ethnic police forces, monitors personal security and freedom of movement of returnees, supervises exhumations and coordinates the search for missing persons. The former Human Rights Field Operation in Rwanda (HRFOR) integrated the spectrum of civil, political, economic, social and cultural rights into all reconstruction activities, which required close coordination between United Nations agencies and donor Governments sponsoring economic and social development programmes. The United Nations is exploring the possibility of creating an intergovernmental body to coordinate all activities in support of Rwandan genocide survivors, especially in the areas of compensation laws and their role as claimants in genocide trials.

Promoting Human Rights Education

The United Nations sees education as a fundamental human right and as a prime means for the promotion of human rights. Human rights education aims at teaching skills, offering knowledge and shaping attitudes, that advance a universal culture of human rights. While human rights education is a global issue, it is effective primarily at the national and local levels. It is through human rights education that the standards established in international human rights law take root in the everyday life of individuals and the local culture of nations. The 1993 Vienna Conference confirmed that human rights education, training and public information were essential for fostering mutual understanding, tolerance and peace among communities.

In assisting Rwanda in its continuing efforts to rebuild its shattered judiciary, the human rights Field Operation concentrated on building and effective judicial system, training judges, prosecutors and other court personnel at all levels of the new justice system. Another strong component of the technical assistance programme was training and human rights education for prison officials and civilian police, including judicial police inspectors, gendarmes and communal police constables.

As of January 1998, an estimated 126,000 detainees were being held in Rwandan prisons or local detention centres, whose combined estimated capacity, according to official sources, was 30,000. With one third of the detainees still waiting to be charged with genocide, the dangerously overcrowded prisons pose a large threat to health, sanitation and security. Armed Hutu extremists have repeatedly targeted detention centres in order to persuade detainees to join them. In May 1998, the

Rwandan Government requested that the Field Operation be suspended until a new agreement revised the mandate, greatly reducing the monitoring functions of HRFOR. The United Nations rejected the limitation and decided to withdraw its observers by the end of July.

Article 12

Freedom from Interference with Privacy, Including Home, Family and Correspondence

United Nations Human rights education campaigns operate at three levels. At the local level, education in human rights provides individuals with practical knowledge about human rights and mechanisms for their protection and the development of their individual potential. At the national and international levels, human rights education promotes values, beliefs and attitudes that inspire action in upholding human rights. Human rights education thus encourages all—from the individual to the international community—to take action to defend human rights and prevent abuses.

The United Nations proclaimed the period 1995-2004 the Decade for Human Rights Education in order to raise awareness of human rights worldwide and to foster a universal culture for human rights. The Decade has been a catalyst for initiatives in some 30 countries to revise school curricula or promote human rights education. To assist States in developing national agendas for human rights education, the United Nations developed a Plan of Action for the Decade and urged governmental and non-governmental authorities to implement the recommendations contained in the plan. The Plan of Action for the Decade for Human Rights Education aims at building effective human rights education programmes and strengthening the role of the mass media. It also encourages the identification of needs and the formulation of educational strategies, the development of educational materials, and the worldwide dissemination of the Universal Declaration.

The United Nations has urged Member States to draw up national plans, with the involvement of a wide range of civil society actors, in order to strengthen human rights education programmes at the national and local levels. To help

States set up national committees for human rights education, the Office of the High Commissioner for Human Rights prepared guidelines for national plans of action for human rights education. In this context, national human rights institutions are considered good focal points for all kinds of local education strategies. They can support school and community teaching, as well as training in the administration of justice, in particular for members of the armed forces and for law enforcement and prison officials. They can also be instrumental in human rights information campaigns and in the creation of documentation centres. United Nations fellowships and training programmes are available to members and staff of national human rights institutions, providing advice on the domestic implementation of international human rights instruments, in the effective investigation of human rights violations and in conflict resolution.

COMBATING DISCRIMINATION

The Horrors of the Mass Extermination of people during the Second World War because of their ethnic origins made it clear to the founders of the United Nations how important it is to protect the human rights of vulnerable groups and to eliminate discrimination. Fifty years later, incidents of genocide and ethnic strife still occur in all parts of the world. Recent violence in Cambodia, Rwanda and the former Yugoslavia, to name only the most notorious conflicts, reminds us that, more than ever, the rights of vulnerable groups need to be protected. Nations face an alarming upsurge of xenophobia and attacks on migrant workers and minorities of all kinds. These are grave dangers not only for the direct victims, but also for societies as a whole, as racism and discrimination engender serious conflict and under mine the overall freedom and prosperity of a community.

Discrimination continues to focus on arbitrarily emphasised differences between individuals and groups. Unfavourable treatment due to ethnic origin, skin colour, gender, language, religion, nationality, class status, political opinion or sexual orientation is a marker of discrimination identified in the Universal Declaration. This marker is applicable today as it was 50 years ago. Widespread discrimination still persists against women. However, recent global trends have also led to new forms of discrimination, particularly directed against immigrant workers. Despite affirmative and punitive legislative measures, there are no quick solutions. Discrimination can be eliminated only through long-term strategies in eradicating poverty, fostering education, empowering women and strengthening accountability—making certain that, worldwide, discrimination will not be tolerated. Until then, groups most vulnerable to discrimination will need special protection.

United Nations efforts to combat discrimination are concentrated in the following areas:

- ❑ Eliminating racism and racial discrimination;
- ❑ Safeguarding the rights of indigenous people;
- ❑ Defending the special rights of all minorities;
- ❑ Promoting the human rights of women;
- ❑ Protecting the rights of children.

Racism

Distinctions and restrictions, preferences and exclusions based on racial prejudice continue to create animosity among people and cause immense suffering and even loss of life. The United Nations combats racial discrimination because of its fundamental injustice. But racial discrimination also represents a serious danger to international peace and security—most contemporary armed conflicts are not of international, but of internal, origin. Just as political doctrines of superiority based on racial differentiation are not only scientifically false but also morally condemnable, the existence of racial barriers is contrary to the notion of open and free societies, harming not only those who are its victims, but also those who discriminate. The United Nations therefore provides leadership in drafting legislation outlawing discrimination and developing policies to combat it effectively. The Office of the United Nations High Commissioner for Human Rights (OHCHR), after reviewing existing national laws against racial discrimination, has drawn up model anti-discrimination legislation concentrating on the following areas:

- Guaranteeing the equality of persons before the law, irrespective of their race, colour nationality or ethnic origin;
- Punishing the dissemination of ideas based on racial superiority and incitement to racial discrimination, as well as racist activities;
- Prohibiting organisations which promote and incite racial discrimination;
- Assuring protection and remedies against acts of racial discrimination.

Article 13

Right to Freedom of Movement and Residence in One's Own Country and to Leave and Return at Will

The United Nations also provides leadership in coordinating international action against discrimination in the fields of education, culture and information. Since 1973, the Organisation has instituted three successive Decades for Action to Combat Racism and Racial Discrimination. The Third Decade to Combat Racism and Racial Discrimination, which began in 1993, provides an important framework for present action against racism. A third World Conference against Racism, Racial Discrimination, Xenophobia and Related Intolerance is planned for the year 2000, offering an opportunity to review progress in the fight against racism and to mobilise effective support at all levels to confront racism and racial discrimination.

In 1993, the Commission on Human Rights appointed a Special Rapporteur on contemporary forms of racism, racial discrimination, xenophobia and related intolerance. In his 1998 report, the Special Rapporteur stated that discrimination against foreigners persisted throughout the world, and was directed particularly against blacks, Arabs and other Muslims,

Jews and the Roma, or Gypsies. Also, studies indicate that discrimination against migrant workers in host countries is on the rise worldwide. The globalisation of international economic relations has prompted many countries to take discriminatory legislative and regulatory measures to protect their domestic labour force, effectively excluding certain categories of immigrants.

One of the most disturbing recent phenomena of racial prejudice, the Special Rapporteur reported, is the upsurge of racist and xenophobic activities on the Internet, with over 100 extremist, especially neo-Nazi, sites advocating white supremacy and inciting racial hatred. Germany and Switzerland have already adopted legislation against the electronic dissemination of racist propaganda. In 1997, a United Nations seminar focused on the role of the Internet in contemporary forms of racism. Reviewing possible responses, such as blocking certain material and prohibiting propaganda on the Internet, participants highlighted the difficulty of finding an effective way to block racist material while protecting the right to free speech.

Indigenous People

Spread across the world from the Arctic to the South Pacific, indigenous people number, at a rough estimate, some 300 million, about 5 per cent of the world's population, still living on the lands of their ancestors, indigenous people are the descendants of the aboriginal populations that inhabited a geographical region at the time when settlers of different cultures or ethnic origins arrived. The new arrivals later came a dominate the region through conquest, occupation or settlement. Retaining social, cultural, economic and political characteristics clearly distinct from those of the other segments of the national populations, indigenous people have become threatened minorities and are perhaps the most vulnerable groups in the world today.

The main threats to the survival of indigenous people arise from the uniqueness of their cultures, the ownership of their lands and their legal status. Although some groups have been relatively successful in retaining their culture, in most parts of the world indigenous people are struggling to maintain their cultural identities and their ways of life. Since 1982, when the United Nations began to formally consider the situation of indigenous people with the establishment of the Working Group on Indigenous Populations, a wide range of activities have been undertaken by the Organisation's human rights programme and by the United Nations system as a whole.

The main areas of concern regarding the human rights of indigenous people are:

- Land rights and indigenous treaties with national Governments;
- Forced displacement and cultural genocide;
- Economic and social marginalisation, including a lack of political representation at the national level;
- Disproportionate impact of unemployment and poverty on indigenous communities;
- Lack of basic health infrastructures and inadequate level of education, with little consideration for indigenous traditional culture in national education programmes;
- Lack of protection for indigenous people's intellectual and cultural poverty, such as knowledge of medicinal plants and preservation of their unique cultural artifacts.

Article 14

Rights to Asylum

The Working Group on Indigenous Populations, a subsidiary organ of the Subcommission on Prevention of Discrimination and Protection of Minorities, consists of five independent experts representing each of the geopolitical regions of the world. Today, the Working Group, whose sessions are open to representatives of indigenous people as well as Governments, United Nations agencies and non-governmental organisations (NGOs), is one of the main international forums in the field of human rights, in charge of reviewing the development of international standards concerning indigenous rights.

The decision that the issue of indigenous rights should be given special consideration led to the long process of drafting a Declaration on the Rights of Indigenous People, beginning in 1985. The draft declaration, concluded in 1993, acknowledges the human rights and fundamental freedoms of indigenous people, including equality, self-determination and non-discrimination. The Declaration, adopted by the Subcommission on Prevention of Discrimination and Protection of Minorities, is now being reviewed by an inter-sessional working group of the Commission on Human Rights.

The General Assembly proclaimed 1993 the International Year of the World's Indigenous People to raise public awareness of indigenous issues and to increase Member States' efforts to protect their rights. Some States with significant indigenous communities, such as Bolivia, Colombia, Norway and Canada, have adopted legislation ensuring that indigenous people become fully involved in their nations' political and economic life. The World Conference on Human Rights further recommended the establishment of a permanent forum for indigenous people within the United Nations system, a proposal which is still being discussed by the Commission on Human Rights. In recent years, however, the concerns of indigenous people have entered the discussions of other forums, particularly their role in sustainable development and the application of their knowledge to biological diversity, desertification and sustainable ecology.

The inauguration of the International Decade of the World's Indigenous People (1995-2004) marked the beginning of a series of promotional activities aimed at strengthening international cooperation for the solution of problems faced by indigenous people in such areas as human rights, the environment, development, education and health. The General

Assembly is working towards the adoption of the Declaration on the Rights of Indigenous People as the most important action of the Decade.

Article 15

Right to a Nationality and Freedom to Change it

OHCHR has created two voluntary funds to assist indigenous people who want to participate in the activities of the Working Group on Indigenous Populations. The Office has also established an Indigenous Fellowship Programme, which offers six months' training on human rights issues and the United Nations system. The programme gives indigenous individuals the opportunity to gain knowledge and skills in the field of international human rights in general, and on indigenous rights in particular, enabling them to assist their local organisations and communities.

Many Governments are aware of the serious problems faced by indigenous people living in their territories and of the factors that make them one of the most vulnerable groups in national societies. In some parts of the world, an ongoing dialogue is taking place. In other places, direct negotiations between indigenous people and Governments have been instituted and are moving forward with the aim of improving relations and guaranteeing better protection of indigenous people's rights.

Minorities

Almost every country has one or more minority groups within its territory, characterised by their own ethnic, linguistic or religious identity, distinct from the majority of the population. Though respect for each group's identity is a great asset to the multicultural diversity of our global society, relations between the majority and a minority as well as among different minorities often cause tensions and violence. In recent years, ethnic, racial and religious tensions have escalated, threatening the economic, social and political fabric of States, as well as their territorial integrity. For this reason, the United

Nations is greatly concerned with human rights issues affecting minorities. Some issues—for instance, demands for independence or autonomy—present a challenge to States that is not always resolved by eliminating discrimination. But meeting the aspirations of various ethnic, religious or linguistic communities and ensuring the rights of minorities significantly lessen tensions among groups and individuals and help to further participatory development, thus contributing to stability and peace.

In the wake of rising discrimination and violence against minority groups, many of whom are demanding greater autonomy, the protection of minorities' rights has attracted the same level of attention as other rights. In 1992, the United Nations adopted the Declaration on the Rights of Persons Belonging to National or Ethnic, Religious and Linguistic Minorities. Because there is no specific reference to minorities in the Universal Declaration of Human Rights, the Declaration emphasizes the special status and rights of minority groups, recognizing the value of preserving their identify, traditions and language. The Declaration spells out the responsibility of States to protect and promote the rights of their minorities by creating favourable conditions for their cultural expression and participation in the economic development of each nation. The Secretary-General has entrusted the High Commissioner for Human Rights with promoting the principles of the Declaration by engaging in continuous dialogue with Governments on behalf of national or ethnic, religious and linguistic minorities. Country visits and reports by Special Rapporteurs are also essential in the implementation of minority-related resolutions.

The tremendous variety of situations among minorities—some are linked by a common cultural heritage, others by geographical closeness—often complicates matters. But it has not precluded United Nations activities promoting human rights standards concerning these vulnerable groups. In 1995, the Subcommission on Prevention of Discrimination and Protection of Minorities established a Working Group on Minorities. The sessions of the Working Group, which are open to representatives of Governments and NGOs involved with the protection of these vulnerable groups, have become the focal point of United Nations activities in the field of minority rights.

Migrant Workers

In recent years, the phenomenon of migration, in the wake of increasing globalization, has affected a large number of States in all regions of the world. Millions of people are now earning their livelihood or looking for paid employment as immigrants in another State. Migrant workers and their families face economic exploitation and discrimination related to labour, as well as low income, poor working standards and a lack of job security. In their quest to cope psychologically and adjust culturally to the host country, they also often suffer from hostile attitudes from the Government, local prejudices and other human rights abuses. These human problems involved in migration are even more serious in cases of irregular or illegal immigration, fuelled by clandestine trafficking in migrant workers.

The number of women migrant workers who have left their country to escape poverty and who suffer inhuman treatment and sexual abuse at the hands of their employers is on the rise. This phenomenon is increasingly recognised as a new form of slavery related to the increase in the trans-national sex trade and trafficking in women and girls. This has prompted the United Nations and the international community to give special attention to the plight of female migrant workers.

Article 16

Right to Marriage and Protection of Family

In 1990, the General Assembly strengthened efforts to recognise the human rights of migrant workers by adopting the International Convention on the Protection of the Rights of All Migrant Workers and Members of Their Families. Besides the core human rights treaties and relevant international labour standards, the Convention takes into account the Slavery Conventions and the United Nations

Educational, Scientific and Cultural Organisation's Convention against Discrimination in Education. At present, the Convention has been ratified by only nine countries and is not yet in force. In 1997, the Commission on Human Rights established a working group of intergovernmental experts on the human rights of minorities to study the status of migrant workers.

Human Rights of Women

Although women constitute a majority of the world's population, there is still no society in which women enjoy full equality with men. In 1996, for example, women held only 7 per cent of ministerial level posts in Governments worldwide. Figures for the number of women in high-level positions in busines and in higher education are similar. Women are still subject to widespread discrimination in everyday life and often lack adequate representation in the public life of developing, as well as developed countries. The United Nations has always affirmed that the promotion of the human rights of women must eliminate all forms of gender-based discrimination and enable them to participate fully in all spheres of civil, political, economic, social and cultural life.

Article 17

Right to own Property

Recognizing the important contribution of women to development and peace, and concerned that in many parts of the world women still did not enjoy equal rights, the United Nations General Assembly proclaimed the period 1976-1985 the United Nations Decade for Women in support of national women's movements around the world. The most significant achievement during the Decade for Women was the adoption (1979) and quick entry into force (1981) of the Convention on the Elimination of All Forms of Discrimination against Women which established the Committee on the Elimination of Discrimination against Women to oversee the implementation of all principles of gender equality and empowerment of women.

National women's movements, in turn, have had a profound impact on the world conferences in this past decade: emphasizing the special needs of the girl child at the Children's Summit in New York (1990); the central role of women in sustainable development at the Earth Summit in Rio de Janeiro (1992); women's reproductive rights at the Population Conference in Cairo (1994); and the special focus on women in the eradication of poverty at the Social Summit in Copenhagen (1995).

Women's movements have also been instrumental in effecting a conceptual shift in emphasis concerning the advancement and empowerment of women. Until the 1980s, the United Nations stressed the recognition of women's rights in order to ensure their full participation in development and to realise non-discrimination. But women's groups advocated, with increasing persuasiveness, that there are no human rights without women's rights, thus grounding the promotion and protection of the rights of women in the universality and indivisibility of all human rights.

This new emphasis, in turn, became the central, cross-cutting theme of the Fourth World Conference on Women in Beijing (1995). Attended by nearly 50,000 participants, the Beijing Conference on Women significantly strengthened the empowerment of women by elaborating the crucial links between the universal advancement of women and social progress around the world. The Beijing Declaration and Platform for Action, Adopted by consensus, highlighted the global nature of human rights issues concerning women and signalled a clear commitment to international norms in gender equality. The Platform for Action advanced a number of forward-looking strategies to integrate a gender perspective into all policies and programmes at all levels and to enhance women's participation in political, civil, economic, social and cultural life. Its multidimensional strategy aims at enabling women to act as autonomous subjects in development and participate in society on their own terms.

The Beijing Declaration elaborates on themes of the Convention on the Elimination of All Forms of Discrimination against Women by recognising that:

- Women's rights are human rights, which need to be protected particularly in relation to violence, sexuality and reproductive health;
- Women should have equal rights in inheriting land and property;
- Women have a special role in the family and in society, but maternity should not impede the full participation of women in society nor should they be penalised for illegal abortions;
- Rape is a war crime, and in some cases and act of genocide, under international humanitarian law.

In the past decade, the United Nations has moved to coordinate its action in advancing the equal status of women by strengthening women's rights throughout the United Nations system, a principle first explicitly expressed at the 1993 Vienna Conference. Its main thrust is to integrate women's concerns into the mainstream of the Organisation so that the protection of women becomes a central concern in all human rights activities and economic and social development programmes.

The 45-member Commission on the Status of women (CSW), established in 1946, is the leading United Nations policy-making body concerned with women's rights and issues affecting the equal status of women. CSW has recently cooperated with the Commission on Human Rights on issues concerning women's human rights. A recent joint project, examining the impact of discrimination against women on their socio-economic status, revealed how gender-specific denial of economic rights directly reduces women's opportunities for social advancement.

Other United Nations programmes are specifically dedicated to the advancement and empowerment of women. The International Research and Training Institute for the Advancement of Women (INSTRAW), established by the Economic and Social Council in 1976, provides training and advisory services for women, especially in developing countries.

INSTRAW is currently promoting the training of women in computer-related communications, and also fostering a more gender-sensitive media.

Article 18

Freedom of Belief and Religion

The United Nations Development Programme (UNDP) has also increasingly focused on the inclusion of women in its development projects, and in 1984 established a fund aimed at strengthening women's economic capacity, the United Nations Development Fund for Women (UNIFEM). UNIFEM offers technical and financial support to women in cooperation with Governments and NGOs and works closely with other United Nations programmes to ensure women's participation in decision-making at all levels of development planning and practice.

Within the United Nations Secretariat, the Division for the Advancement of Women (DAW) and the Secretary-General's Special Adviser on Gender Issues and the Advancement of Women monitor the progress in women's full enjoyment of their rights in the light of the goals set by the Beijing Platform for Action. The Division also plays an important role in supporting the Committee on the Elimination of Discrimination against Women. DAW, UNIFEM and INSTRAW have jointly set up an important UN Internet getway on the advancement and empowerment of women titled "Women Watch".

Within the United Nations system, the Office of the United Nations High Commissioner for Refugees (UNHCR), the World Health Organisation (WHO) and the International Labour Organisation (ILO) have also taken significant steps towards integrating women rights issues and a gender perspective into their activities. The mandate of the United Nations Children's Fund (UNICEF) has always been oriented to the well-being of women in their role as mothers, with activities to combat malnutrition, maternal mortality, gender-based violence and unequal access to education. One important UNICEF programme aims at eliminating the sexual exploitation of girls by providing basic education and employment counselling for girls at risk.

Violence Against Women

According to the 1997 UNICEF report *The Progress of Nations,* violence against women and girls is the most pervasive violation of human rights in the world today. Cutting across economic, social, cultural and religious barriers, violence against women is an insidious phenomenon affecting the lives of millions of women and taking a dismaying variety of forms. The international community did not take concrete action against the alarming global dimensions of gender-based violence until 1993, when the General Assembly adopted the Declaration on the Elimination of Violence against Women. Until that point, most Governments tended to regard violence against women largely as a private matter between individuals, and not as a pervasive human rights problem requiring active State intervention.

The Declaration defines violence against women as "any act of gender-based violence that results in, or is likely to result in, physical, sexual or psychological harm or suffering to women, including threats of such acts, coercion or arbitrary deprivation of liberty, whether occurring in public or in private life". It also identifies systematic rape, sexual slavery and forced pregnancy of women in situations of armed conflicts as extremely grave violations of the fundamental principles of human rights and international humanitarian law. The Declaration identifies three areas in which women are particularly vulnerable:

- Violence in the family;
- Violence within the community;
- Violence perpetrated or condoned by the State.

Article 19

Freedom of Opinion and Information

In the family, domestic violence is on the increase, according to a World Bank study, which found that, worldwide,

25 to 50 per cent of all women suffer physical abuse by their partner. An estimated 60 million females die because of son-preference; many parents, hoping for sons, kill or neglect their daughters before or shortly after birth. Each year, an estimated 2 million girls in at least 28 countries are subjected to the traumatizing traditional practice of female genital mutilation. In some societies, girls are compelled to marry at an early age before they are physically, mentally or emotionally mature.

In the community, rape continues to be a widespread offence that still brings shame and blame onto the innocent victims. Women who are victims of rape and sexual harassment often suffer trauma, physical handicap or even death. The extent of trafficking in women and girls, within and across borders, has reached alarming proportions, especially in Asian and Eastern European countries. At the same time sex tourism to developing countries is a well-organised industry in several Western and other developed countries.

In cases of State-perpetrated or condoned violence, police or prison officials, who supposedly protect women from violence, are often perpetrators of sexual abuse. Thousand, of women held in custody are routinely raped in police detention centres worldwide and cruelly tortured by security forces. In virtually all armed conflicts, rape continues to be widely used as a cynical tactic to subjugate and terrify entire communities. Women and girl children are frequently victims of gang rape and sexual slavery at the hands of soldiers, as seen during the conflicts in Rwanda and the former Yugoslavia and in many other conflicts around the world.

Article 20

Right to Peaceful Assembly and Association

The United Nations is committed to combating violence against women by addressing the root causes of the problem as well as treating its manifestations, challenging the ways in which gender roles and unequal power relations are articulated in society. Because most laws fail to protect victims or to punish perpetrators, it is crucial to enforce laws that redefine the limits of acceptable behaviour and to eliminate the prevailing culture of impunity by applying standards of "due diligence" for Governments. At the same time, information campaigns emphasizing the equal rights of women must address society at large, educating judges and police officers, as well as boys and men in general, in order to change the social attitudes and beliefs that tolerate violence against women.

Changing people's attitudes and mentality towards women will take a long time. But raising awareness of the issue of violence against women and educating boys and men to view women as equal partners in private and public life are crucial to democratizing society and are as important as taking legal steps to ensure the protection of women's rights. This will require sustained collaboration between governmental and non-governmental actors, including educators, health-care authorities, legislators, the judiciary and the mass media.

The United Nations is mobilizing concerted international initiatives to protect women from violence at the local and national levels. The 1993 World Conference on Human Rights urged Governments and the United Nations system to work together towards banning all forms of sexual harassment and exploitation. The Vienna Declaration highlighted as areas of critical concern international trafficking, cultural prejudices and religious extremism, as well as gender bias in the administration of justice and in all aspects of political, civil, economic, social and cultural life. Since 1994, the Special Rapporteur on violence against women, in concert with other special rapporteurs of the Commission on Human Rights, has been drawing increasing political attention to the causes and consequences of gender-related violence, recommending measures to eliminate its occurrence and to remedy its consequences. The Special Rapporteur has carried out missions on military and sexual slavery in wartime in Korea and Japan; trafficking in women and girls in Poland; domestic violence in Brazil; rape in South Africa; violence against women in armed conflicts in Rwanda; and violence against women in prisons in the United States.

Monitoring and reporting on violations are essential tools for protecting women's rights. The experts of the Commission on Human Rights and the treaty bodies are increasingly integrating a gender perspective into their work and now generally devote a separate section of their reports to the analysis of discrimination that women still face. Besides the Special Rapporteur on violence against women, some of the thematic mandates, such as executions, torture, religious intolerance, freedom of opinion and expression, racial discrimination and independence of the judiciary, are also concerned with women's rights and are required to fully integrate these concerns in their reports.

Protecting the Rights of Children

Two billion people in the world today are under the age of 18. As the most vulnerable members of a society; children are often victims of serious human rights violations. The extent of systematic abuses against children is disturbing, ranging from malnutrition to military recruitment, from labour exploitation to lack of education, with lifelong implications for their well-being as adults.

Article 21

Right to Participate in Government and in Free Elections and to Equal Access to Public Service

Malnutrition is by far the most pernicious abuse against children in the world. Each year, more than 12 million children under the age of five die in developing countries. More than 55 per cent of all child deaths worldwide can be attributed to malnutrition. Some 40 million babies, one out of three born each year, are at risk simply because they are not registered at birth. Without a birth certificate, a child is not officially recognised as a citizen and is often denied adequate access to basic health services and primary education. At least 120 million children between the ages of 5 and 14 work full time, according to ILO, and for about 250 million children work is a secondary activity. Other threats to children's lives and development throughout the world include murder of street children, sale of organs, child pornography and prostitution. More than 2 million children are believed to be involved in prostitution, including some 1 million in Asia and 300,000 in the United States.

Protection and promotion of the rights of rights of children have always been a central issue on the agenda of the United Nations. Slow but steady progress has been made towards the affirmation that children like adults, are the subject of rights, and not only helpless objects of concern or beneficiaries of services. In 1959, the Declaration of the Rights of the Child represented the first concrete affirmation by the international community that children needed special protection and, for the first time, defined a child as a person below the age of 18.

The International Year of the Child in 1979 marked the starting point of the debates that led to the formulation of the Convention on the Rights of the Child, which was adopted unanimously in 1989. Setting common standards for the protection of the rights of children within different cultural settings, the Convention is today the most widely ratified instrument in the field of human rights, with a total of 191 States parties. Reaffirming the principles of the International Bill of Human Rights, the Convention emphasises particularly the right to life, survival and development of children. The main principles outlined in the Convention are non-discrimination, the child's best interests and the views of the child. These last two concepts reflect recent awareness of the importance of recognising a child's own needs and opinions within a society.

The Convention provides the framework that serves as a catalyst and guideline for action at the national level. It sets universal standards to which each country should conform its laws with respect to its specific cultural situation. The Committee on the Rights of the Child, composed of 10 international experts, was convened for the first time in 1991. Its main role is to monitor the implementation of the Convention by examining regular mandatory reports submitted by States parties. While some countries lag behind in submitting their reports and others provide insufficient data, there has been great progress in the implementation of the national plans of action.

In 1990, the World Summit for Children in New York reaffirmed the standards established by the Convention and adopted the World Declaration on the Survival, Protection and Development of Children, setting the year 2000 as the deadline for the successful implementation of benchmarks benefiting the lives and development of children:

- ❑ Reduction of the infant mortality rate by one third or at least to under 50 per 1,000 live births and reduction of the maternal mortality rate by half;
- ❑ Reduction of severe and moderate malnutrition among under-five children by half;
- ❑ Universal access to safe drinking water and to adequate sanitation;
- ❑ Universal access to basic education and completion of primary education by at least 80 per cent of primary-school-age children;
- ❑ Reduction of the adult illiteracy rate to no more than half its 1990 level, with emphasis on female literacy.

The Summit developed a Plan of Action that called for various activities on behalf of the well-being of children and mobilised international cooperation among Governments, NGOs, the media and civil society. At the national level, each country is urged to review its budget to ensure that programmes aimed at the protection of children's rights receive priority when resources are allocated.

Guided by the Convention on the Rights of the Child, UNICEF promotes sustainable development for children and strives to establish children's rights as enduring ethical principles and international standards of behaviour towards children. Working together with other United Nations agencies, Governments and NGOs, UNICEF provides low-cost, community-based services in primary health care, nutrition, basic education and sanitation as a way to protect the rights of the child in the developing world. UNICEF's annual reports *The State of the World's Children and The Progress of Nations* review steps undertaken by States parties to meet the goals of the Convention and promote the well-being of children.

Article 22

Right to Social Security

The United Nations machinery in the field of children's rights comprises a variety of bodies, among which the Committee on the Rights of the Child plays a central role. The Special Rapporteur on the sale of children, child prostitution and child pornography analyses instances of sexual exploitation of children in various countries. A working group of the Commission on Human Rights is drafting an optional protocol to the Convention on the Rights of the Child on the sale of children, child prostitution and child pornography.

Children and Armed Conflict

Children all over the world continue to be victims of the wars of adults—losing parents, families and homes, losing their childhood and the opportunity for education, losing limbs and their lives to armed conflicts. In the past decade alone, an estimated 2 million children have been killed in armed conflicts. Three times as many have been seriously injured to permanently disabled. One million have been orphaned. Countless others have been forced to witness or even take part in horrifying acts of violence. A 1995 UNICEF survey of more than 3,000 children in Rwanda, in the aftermath of the genocidal killings of the previous year, found that more than 80 per cent had lost immediate family members, and more than one third had actually witnessed the murders.

The direct physical effects and the collateral psychosocial damage endured by children during armed conflicts are devastating to their future development. One of the most alarming trends in armed conflicts is the forced recruitment of young children as active soldiers. Some are conscripted, others kidnapped or forced to join armed groups to defend their families. They are sometimes used as advance scouts or mine detectors. In cases of acute hunger and poverty, parents sometimes offer their children for service or, if marriage prospects are poor, encourage their daughters to become soldiers. An estimated 500,000 children are currently involved in armed conflicts around the world.

Article 23

Right to Work and Fair Pay for Work

Modern warfare often brutally uproots children because their families are forced to flee to neighbouring States or are internally displaced within their own countries. Of the world's estimated 22 million refugees and 30 million displaced people, half are children. Displacement has a profound physical, emotional and developmental impact on children and sharply increases their vulnerability. Wandering around as refugees, often separated from their families, these children are continually threatened by sudden attacks, shelling and landmines.

Rape and sexual exploitation are a continual threat in armed conflicts. Girls, in particular, are subject to gender-based violence, such as sexual abuse and mutilation, prostitution and trafficking. The widespread practice of rape by armed forces often has a tragic ripple effect that extends far beyond the immediate pain and degradation. Sexual abuse can lead to sexually transmitted diseases and HIV/AIDS infection. Rape victims who become pregnant are often ostracised by their families and communities and forced to abandon their unwanted babies. In such unbearable circumstances, many of these girls commit suicide out of despair.

In addition to the fragmenting of family and community, the breakdown of infrastructure and disruption of education due to armed conflicts have devastating long-term effects on the future of children. The destruction of schools and education networks represents one of the greatest developmental setbacks for countries affected by armed conflict. Missed education and lost vocational skills take years to replace, making the overall task of post-conflict recovery even more difficult.

Since the 1990 World Summit on Children, the United Nations has placed the plight of children affected by armed conflicts high on the international agenda. The United Nations report *Impact of Armed Conflict on Children* (1996) provided the first comprehensive assessment of the multiple ways in which children are abused and brutalised in the context of war. In 1997, in response to the urgent need for a public advocate on behalf of children's rights in situations of armed conflict, the Secretary-General appointed a Special Representative for Children in Armed Conflict. A working group is also drafting an Optional Protocol to the Convention on the Rights of the Child on Involvement of Children in Armed Conflicts, which seeks to raise the minimum age of recruitment into armed forces to 18 and to specify measures for demobilisation and reintegratioon of child soldiers into society.

HUMAN RIGHTS AND CONFLICTS

Today, some of the most serious threats to international peace and security are armed conflicts that arise, not among nations, but among warring factions within a State. Although situations of internal violence, they often spill over borders, endangering the security of other States and resulting in complex humanitarian emergencies. The human rights abuses prevalent in internal conflicts are now among the most atrocious in the world. In 1996, there were 19 ongoing situations of internal violence around the world in which 1,000 people or more were killed. These so-called "high-intensity conflicts" cumulatively led to between 6.5 million and 8.5 million deaths. In the same year, there were also 40 "low-intensity conflicts", each causing between 100 and 1,000 deaths. Another 2 million deaths can be added to these figures if one includes situations of internal violence that had de-escalated in 1996.

The number of conflict-related deaths is only a small indication of the tremendous amount of suffering, displacement and devastation caused by conflicts. Assaults on the fundamental right to life are widespread—massacres, indiscriminate attacks on civilians, executions of prisoners, starvation of entire population. Torture is common in internal conflicts, as are measures restricting people's freedom of movement—forcible relocations, mass expulsions, denial of the right to seek asylum or the right to return to one's home. Women and girls are raped by soldiers and forced into prostitution, and children are abducted to serve as soldiers. Tens of thousands of people detained in connection with conflicts "disappear" each year, usually killed and buried in secret, leaving their families with the torment of not knowing their fate. Thousands of others are arbitrarily imprisoned and never brought to trial or, if they are, are subject to grossly unfair procedures. Homes, schools and hospitals are deliberately destroyed. Relief convoys, which try to assist civilians by providing humanitarian aid, are attacked.

The denial of fundamental rights relating to employment, housing, food or the respect for cultural life and large-scale discrimination and exclusion from the decision-making processes of society are the root causes of many grave crises today. Armed conflicts clearly illustrate the indivisibility and interdependence of all human rights. The collapse of infrastructure and civic institutions undermines the range of civil, economic, political and social rights. The rights to adequate health, housing, education, freedom of movement and expression, privacy and fair trial are only some of the fundamental rights and freedoms affected when hospitals and schools are closed, water and sanitation polluted, local administrations unable to function, and police and judicial systems shattered or corrupted. Government institutions often become increasingly militarised, with the armed forces assuming civilian policing functions and military courts trying civilians. Prolonged conflicts also affect rural areas; crops are destroyed, crippling productivity in subsistence farming and agriculture and leading to chronic food shortages, malnutrition and famines. Ill health and poverty are often the most devastating long-term consequences of conflicts.

Human Rights and the Transition to Peace

The 1993 World Conference on Human Rights affirmed the crucial connection between international peace and security and the rule of law and human rights, placing them all within the larger context of democratisation and development. The need to reinforce these vital links has been highlighted by the sharp increase in bloody conflicts and man-made calamities in this decade.

The United Nations is increasingly combining efforts to prevent or end conflicts with measures aimed at reducing human rights abuses in situations of internal violence. Special emphasis is placed on ensuring the protection of minorities, strengthening democratic institutions, realizing the right to development and securing universal respect for human rights. Preventing massive human rights violations from arising, responding to violations before they escalate into conflicts and controlling and resolving conflicts before they escalate further are central concerns of preventive action. In the context of preventive action and peacemaking, the Security Council and the Secretary-General, in carrying out his "good offices", are also assisted by the Department of Political Affairs (DPA).

Recognising that human rights violations are frequently the root causes of conflict and humanitarian crises, the United Nations is making efforts towards strengthening its early warning capacity and response to conflicts by integrating human rights monitoring into peacekeeping operations, thus enhancing its ability to deal with allegations of human rights violations. The Office of the High Commissioner for Human Rights is developing close contacts with the United Nations departments, offices and programmes responsible for peacekeeping and for humanitarian assistance, in particular the Department of Peacekeeping Operations (DPKO), DPA, the Office for the Coordination of Humanitarian Affairs (OCHA) and the Office of the United Nations High Commissioner for Refugees (UNHCR).

The human rights programme is performing a crucial role not only in the United Nations early warning system, but also in post-conflict reconstruction, building mutual confidence and helping to re-establish a climate of understanding. The international community has recognised that protecting human rights in the aftermath of conflicts cannot be isolated from how the conflict is brought to an end. Experience in assisting countries in transition to democracy has shown how important the inclusion of human rights provisions in peace or transitional agreements can be.

Article 24

Right to Rest and Leisure

In recent years beginning with the El Salvador mission in 1990, a number of peacekeeping and other political operations have included a human rights component. A human rights field presence was part of the peace processes in Cambodia, El Salvador, Guatemala and Haiti. The International Civilian Mission in Haiti, for example, has been dedicated to verifying the respect for human rights since its inception in February 1993. After the return to constitutional order in October 1994, the Mission expanded its work to include the promotion of human rights, civic education, electoral assistance and institution-building. It supports the National Truth and Justice Commission and assists in the strengthening of the Haitian judical and penal system.

The human rights missions in El Salvador and Guatemala demonstrate the crucial role of human rights in rebuilding trust and fostering a climate of reconciliation after armed conflict. In Guatemala, the Human Rights Verification Mission (MINUGUA) was deployed in 1994, two years in advance of the final peace agreement signed by the Government and the opposition front. The largest United Nations human rights verification mission ever mounted, with 13 regional and subregional offices and 254 international staff, MINUGUA's field presence is more extensive than that of many national institutions in Guatemala. In the past two years, the Mission has successively reported dramatic declines in verified complaints of torture, forced disappearances and arbitrary detention.

The High Commissioner for Human Rights has deployed human Rights field operations in Burundi, Rwanda, the former Yugoslavia and the Democratic Republic of the Congo (formerly Zaire). In each case, following up allegations of violations and establishing a framework of respect for human rights were seen as part and parcel of the work of creating an atmosphere of trust in a post-conflict situation. This has been a vital lesson for the United Nations in the 1990s.

Article 25

Right to Adequate Standard of Living for Health and Well-being

Developing Fundamental Humanitarian Standards

Just as human rights are a key element in peacekeeping and peace-building efforts, the protection of human rights is also recognised as a priority in humanitarian operations. The United Nations is currently leading efforts to establish minimum humanitarian standards, seeking to identify fundamental rules of human rights and humanitarian law that can be applied in all circumstances, in times of conflict, as well as in situations of mass exodus, for the protection of human rights. These efforts aim to provide the human rights framework necessary to find long-term solutions to the root causes of conflict and to prevent the excesses that make reconciliation so difficult. The United Nations urges national authorities to respect international human rights standards in such situations. But one of the most pressing problems now is enforcing accountability of non-State actors committing crimes against humanity. For these reasons, the United Nations is incorporating human rights concerns into all aspects of its response to conflicts—from preventive action to humanitarian assistance.

For the United Nations, providing assistance to the victims of conflict is the supreme humanitarian task. Though not traditionally considered a human rights function, there is no doubt that the provision of food, medical care and basic education is a direct and tangible means of supporting the human dignity of the affected population. The human rights framework can also help to set the parameters and rules for the delivery of humanitarian assistance—ensuring the non-discriminatory treatment of those in need, and paying due regard to the special needs of women and children.

Refugees are particularly vulnerable to the loss of human rights. The violation of fundamental rights is almost always the root cause of refugee flows. Displacement and forced migration are intrinsically human rights issues, underlying related questions such as mass exoduses, the status of internally displaced persons and the right to return to their homes and communities. Since it began its work in 1951, UNHCR has always incorporated a human rights dimension into humanitarian action, particularly concerning the rights to asylum and non-forced repatriation. Its work has been based on the 1951 Convention relating to the Status of Refugees and its 1967 Protocol, which define the rights and duties of refugees. Durable solutions to these man-made catastrophes require sustained and concerted efforts towards reconstruction and reconciliation. The challenge of ensuring the sustainability of return extends far beyond the capacities of any single organisation and requires the creative collaboration of a variety of actors. For this reason, the High Commissioner for Human Rights and the High Commissioner for Refugees are expanding the cooperation of their offices, on both an informal and a formal basis, through the day-to-day contracts among the staff, at Headquarters and in the field. Their interaction, guided by a Memorandum of Understanding, includes joint meetings and projects, as well as facilitating the sharing of responsibilities by exchanging personnel and co-sponsoring staff training.

The Office of the United Nations High Commissioner for Human Rights also works closely with OCHA, the central Secretariat body responsible for coordinating United Nations humanitarian action. The increased collaboration between the two offices seeks to provide relief for victims of humanitarian disasters within an integrated framework of human rights law and humanitarian law. In order to ensure that their work is harmonised, the High Commissioner for Human Rights participates in the meetings of the Executive Committee on Humanitarian Affairs and the Inter-Agency Standing

Committee, the main coordinating forums for developing humanitarian programmes and formulating strategic policies.

Article 26

Right to Education

A Rights-based Approach to Peace-building

Just as human rights forge vital links between peace, democracy and development, bringing the full weight of the United Nations human rights programme to bear can also facilitate the successful transition between peacekeeping operations and humanitarian emergency assistance to long-term peace-building and sustainable development. Societies that are emerging from civil conflict have particular needs in the area of human rights and economic development. The complexities of post-conflict situations require that special attention be given to repairing the large-scale damage inflicted on economic, health and educational infrastructures. But international development programmes can also contribute to healing the psychological scars of conflict. Strengthening respect for human rights through development contributes to a climate of confidence that helps a society regain its equilibrium.

Such a human rights framework is most effectively realised when United Nations operations overseeing or implementing peace agreements incorporate human rights specialists, both in their monitoring capacity as human rights observers and as technical advisers, to help strengthen the administration of justice. The United Nations is developing a two-track approach in which immediate humanitarian assistance and long-term development assistance eventually converge, with human rights a crucial binding element in both. This means that the various actors, from international institutions developing projects to individuals operating in the field, must work together, aware of the common goals and mutual needs of the parallel programmes. As demonstrated in Cambodia, El Salvador, Haiti and Rwanda, work in the field demands a delicate mix of standard-setting, training, advice on laws and procedures, and funding. United Nations human rights experts assist in building an independent judiciary and in training police and security personnel in human rights standards for law enforcement. They also provide guidance in drafting press freedom laws, minority legislation or laws securing women's equality.

Without prescribing for any one society a preferred model of economic development or cultural organisation the rights-based approach to peace-building facilitates the growth of civil society. Human rights standards provide the impartial means through which reconciliation can be achieved. A human rights framework provides certain guarantees for justice and also protects against random retribution, establishing the parameters within which democratic societies can legitimately balance the interests of the victims against larger concerns for social harmony.

Breaking the Cycle of Impunity

Solving conflicts also means addressing past abuses, especially against the civilian population. A recurring theme that applies to all human rights abuses in conflicts is that again and again the members of armed groups kill, torture, rape or attack civilians with virtual impunity, apparently confident that they will never be called to account for their crimes. Impunity is a relatively new concept for an age-old phenomenon of injustice, namely, the absence of penalties or inadequacy of compensation for massive and grave violations of human rights. The manner in which a Government reacts to human rights violations committed by its agents, through action or omission, clearly shows the degree of its willingness to ensure effective protection of human rights. Very often, a government's declared commitment to respect human rights is contradicted in practice by an alternating cycle of violations and impunity. In some cases, impunity is inscribed in legislation that exempts perpetrators of human rights abuses from prosecution. In other cases, despite the existence of legal provisions for the prosecution of human rights violators, impunity continues in practice. Authorities often do not react to complaints filed by victims, their families or representatives, or to urgent appeals by United Nations special rapporteurs.

Problems related to the independent and impartial functioning of the judiciary have also encouraged impunity. Although Governments are under an obligation to initiate inquiries into allegations as soon as they are brought to their attention, in some countries impartial investigations are rarely conducted. In other cases, public inquiries are compromised, with light sentences imposed on perpetrators despite the gravity of the crimes committed. In particular, trials of members of the security forces before military courts are sometimes undermined by an ill-conceived *esprit de corps*. There are also instances where low-ranking officials are convicted of human rights violations or crimes, while those in positions of command escape responsibility. Often victims—and sometimes witnesses who assist in investigative efforts—are subjected to intimidation and death threats.

For this reason, the United Nations has intensified efforts to bring the perpetrators of such crimes to justice and break the cycle of impunity. Ensuring that individuals are held criminally responsible and punished for committing serious human rights abuses is one of the most effective means of dealing with grave injustice and fostering necessary reconciliation. In countries where the justice system does not function properly, legislative reforms are required first, before the judiciary can effectively undertake investigations. In cases where violations warrant particular treatment because of their special nature or gravity, as with apartheid in South Africa for example, Governments may establish special truth commissions adhering to the same requirements of independence, impartiality and competence as ordinary courts. The results of their investigations can be made public, and sometimes their recommendations are binding on the authorities.

Article 27

Right to Participate in the Cultural Life of the Community

The history of impunity parallels the struggle of civil society against authoritarian States. During the 1970s, the

United Nations began to take action in the campaign against impunity after non-governmental organisations and human rights groups pioneered the creation of an international strategy to address the widespread problem. In the absence of an international criminal court, prominent "courts of opinion" sometimes filled an institutional gap in international human rights law. In the 1980s, the proliferation of "amnesty" laws proclaimed by military dictatorships anxious to arrange their own permanent impunity while still in power provoked a strong reaction from victims, who undertook legal campaigns to ensure that justice was done.

In the 1990s, with the end of the cold war and the restoration of democracy in many parts of the world, the question of impunity within the context of national reconciliation became a matter of international concern. When, in the course of democratisation, the former victims took over the responsibility of the State, they often found themselves forced to moderate their initial commitment against impunity in the name of national reconciliation. But the Inter-American Court of Human Rights, in a recent ground-breaking ruling, found that amnesty for the perpetrators of serious human rights violations was incompatible with the right of every individual to a fair hearing before an impartial and independent court.

In 1997, two experts of the Subcommission on Prevention of Discrimination and Protection of Minorities presented reports on impunity, one in relation to civil and political rights, the other concerning economic, social and cultural rights. The reports propose a draft "set of principles for the promotion and protection of human rights through action to combat impunity". The principles refer to victims' legal rights as obligations of society, particularly the right to know, the right to justice and the right to reparations. If adopted by the General Assembly, these guiding principles would provide the strategic framework for the international campaign against impunity.

Towards an International Criminal Court

In 1945, at the Tribunal of Nuremberg, which judged the accused war criminals of Nazi Germany, the international community pledged that "never again" would it allow monstrous crimes against humanity or genocide to take place. For nearly half a century, the United Nations has recognised the need for a world court to prosecute and punish persons responsible for crimes of international concern, such as genocide, crimes against humanity, war crimes and the crime of aggression. In 1948, the United Nations General Assembly adopted the Convention on the Prevention and Punishment of the Crime of Genocide, one day before adopting the Universal Declaration of Human Rights. In 1949, a Diplomatic Conference for the Establishment of International Conventions for the Protection of Victims of War, held in Geneva from 21 April to 12 August, adopted four Conventions, which codified the humanitarian action of soldiers in times of war. The four Geneva Conventions outlined the human treatment of wounded, sick or surrendering combatants, prisoners and civilians, and banned the wilful taking and killing of hostages. By 1951, these international treaties against genocide, war crimes and crimes against humanity had entered into force, establishing a body of law known as International Humanitarian Law. The United Nations directed the International Law Commission to draft a statute for an International Criminal Court. But for a long time disagreement among Member States on the jurisdiction of such a court hindered any decisive development towards its creation.

The atrocities that occurred in the former Yugoslavia and Rwanda were widely seen as failures of the international community to intervene in time to prevent serious human rights violations. However, Yugoslavia and Rwanda are not unique as conflict areas where massive violations of human rights and international humanitarian law occurred. In recent decades, there have been many instances of crimes against humanity committed in war for which no individuals have been held accountable. In Cambodia in the 1970s, for example, the Khmer Rough killed over 1 million people. In many countries around the world, massacres of civilians, including countless women and children, continue to this day.

International Criminal Tribunal for the Former Yugoslavia

In 1993, faced with widespread atrocities committed under

the policy of "ethnic cleansing" during the Yugoslav conflict between the Muslim, Serb and Croatian communities, the United Nations responded by setting up an international tribunal to bring the perpetrators of the crimes to justice. In May 1993, the Security Council, acting under Chapter VII of the United Nations Charter, created the International Tribunal for the Prosecution of Persons Responsible for Serious Violations of International Humanitarian Law Committed in the Territory of the Former Yugoslavia since 1991 (ICTY). The Tribunal highlighted the need for a permanent International Criminal Court to deal with such violations quickly and effectively.

The Tribunal, which has its seat at The Hague, the Netherlands, was given the broadest mandate of any international investigative body since the Nuremberg trials. Its statute defines the Tribunal's authority to prosecute individuals responsible for four groups of offences: grave breaches of the Geneva Conventions of 1949; violations of the laws or customs of war; genocide; and crimes against humanity. Moreover, because the Tribunal was established under Chapter VII of the United Nations Charter, the Security Council can use sanctions and other measures to enforce the Tribunal's decisions.

Crimes Against Humanity

Genocide refers to acts committed with intent to destroy, in whole or in part, a national, ethnical, racial or religious group, by either killing or causing serious bodily or mental harm to members of the group. Genocide also includes deliberately imposing living conditions calculated to bring about the group's physical destruction, such as imposing measures intended to prevent births or forcibly transferring children of the group.

Crimes against humanity are acts deliberately committed as part of a widespread or systematic attack directed against any civilian population. Crimes include murder and extermination (the intentional deprivation of access to food and medicine, calculated to bring about the destruction of part of a population). Crimes against humanity also include the deportation or forcible transfer of people and inhumane imprisonment in violation of fundamental rules of international law. Persecution of any identifiable group or collectivity on political, racial, national, ethnic, cultural, religious, gender or other grounds is also universally recognised as impermissible under international law. This applies also to the enforced disappearance of persons, the crime of apartheid and other inhumane acts causing serious physical injury or great suffering.

War crimes are grave breaches of the 1949 Geneva Conventions. Serious violations of the laws and customs of war include intentionally directing attacks against the civilian population not taking direct part in hostilities or deporting the population of an occupied territory; employing weapons, material and methods of warfare which cause superfluous injury or unnecessary suffering or which are inherently indiscriminate in violation of the international law of armed conflict, such as biological, chemical and nuclear weapons; sexual slavery, enforced prostitution, forced pregnancy, enforced sterilization, or any other form of sexual violence; and the conscription or enlistment of children under the age of 15 years into armed forces or groups participating in hostilities.

Article 28

Right to Social Order Assuring Human Rights

To date, 60 individuals have been publicly indicted, and 28 of the accused apprehended. Five trials are ongoing before the Tribunal and two verdicts have been handed down. One individual was found guilty of crimes against humanity and sentenced to 20 years' imprisonment. In the other case, the accused pleaded guilty to war crimes and was sentenced to five years' imprisonment.

The Tribunal has primacy over national jurisdictions and can issue an international arrest warrant if national authorities are unwilling to cooperate or fail to serve the initial indictment of the accused individuals. The Tribunal then notifies the Security Council to enforce the warrant. By the middle of 1998, eight international arrest warrants had been issued. The attempts by the Tribunal to arrest indicted persons currently living in the federal Republic of Yugoslavia have been generally without success. The Government has consistently refused to meet its international obligations to hand over those indicted for war crimes and crimes against humanity.

Article 29

Responsibility to Community Essential to Free and Full Development of the Individual

International Criminal Tribunal for Rwanda

In Rwanda, civil strife and internal violence led to genocide on a vast scale. From April to July 1994, a systematically planned genocide by extremist Hutu militia claimed the lives of between 500,000 and 1 million persons. The main victims of this carnage were members of the Tutsi minority and moderate Hutus. The civil war forced hundreds of thousands of Rwandans to flee to neighbouring countries. By mid-July, more than 2 million Rwandan refugees were living in camps in Burundi, Tanzania and Zaire. Many thousands more had been displaced internally within the territory of Rwanda.

In November 1994, the Security Council created the International Criminal Tribunal for the Prosecution of Persons Responsible for Genocide and Other Serious Violations of International Humanitarian Law Committed in the Territory of Rwanda (ICTR). The Tribunal also prosecutes Rwandan citizens responsible for genocide, crimes against humanity and war crimes committed in the territory of neighbouring States between 1 January 1994 and 31 December 1994.

While the Hague Tribunal consists of two chambers and an appeals chamber, the International Criminal Tribunal for Rwanda, which has its seat in Arusha, Tanzania, recently added a third chamber to accelerate the procedural process. The Chief Prosecutor, based in The Hague, serves for both Tribunals.

The International Criminal Tribunal for Rwanda issued its first indictment in November 1995. By 1998, three trials had commenced. As of August 1998, 35 indicted individuals were in custody in Arusha

One of the most dramatic cases so far before the Tribunal has been the trial of Rwandan ex-Prime Minister Jean Kambanda. In his long-delayed, first appearance before the Tribunal on 1 May 1998, Kambanda pleaded guilty to the crime of genocide. This is the first time in history that an accused individual publicly confessed to the crime of genocide. The former Prime Minister was subsequent sentenced to life in prison, also the first-ever conviction of an individual for the crime of genocide.

In a related trial, the former mayor of the Rwandan District of Taba, Jean-Pierre Akayesu, was convicted on 2 September 1998 of genocide against Tutsi citizens, as well as for the crimes of rape, torture and other inhumane acts and subsequently sentenced to life imprisonment.

Establishing the International Criminal Court

The International Criminal Court (ICC) was finally created at the United Nations Diplomatic Conference of Plenipotentiaries on the Establishment of an International Criminal Court, held in Rome from 15 June to 17 July 1998. Delegations from 160 countries, 17 intergovernmental organisations, 14 United Nations specialised agencies and funds and 124 NGOs participated in the five-week landmark Conference. The Rome Statute of the International Criminal Court was adopted by a vote of 120 in favour to 7 against, with 21 abstentions. The treaty establishing the Court needs to be ratified by at least 60 States parties before entering into force.

The establishment of the Court makes it clear that the international community no longer tolerates violations of human rights without assigning responsibility. Unlike the ad hoc Tribunals, the Court provides a comprehensive mechanism for punishing perpetrators of genocide and other crimes against humanity. The assurance that at least some perpetrators of war crimes, crimes against humanity or genocide may be brought to justice acts as a significant deterrent, and in itself may provide incentives to end conflicts.

The ICC forges a mission link in the international legal order, for the International Court of Justice (ICJ) at The Hague handles only cases between States. The ICC will act on the principle of individual responsibility, applied equally and without exception to any individual throughout a governmental hierarchy or military chain of command. The appropriate punishment would apply to heads of State and commanding officers, as well as to low-ranking soldiers in the field or militia recruits. Especially in situations of internal violence, in countries where there is no legitimate Government, ensuring accountability at the international level is cruical.

The Court, comprising the Presidency, a Trial Division, a Pre-Trial Division, an Appeals Division, the Office of the Prosecutor and the Registry, will be located at the Hague in the Netherlands, but may convene elsewhere if necessary. The Assembly of States parties elects the Court's Prosecutor and 18 judges for terms limited to nine years, with no two judges of the same nationality. The judges, in turn, elect the President. The Asembly of States parties will define the precise nature of the Court's relationship with the United Nations at a later stage. The maximum penalty the Court can impose is life imprisonment.

The International Criminal Court will complement national criminal courts, which should normally try alleged criminals within their jurisdiction. The Court is needed only when national institutions have collapsed due to conflict (as in Rwanda) or when a State is unwilling to try its own nationals (as in the former Yugoslavia). The Prosecutor has the power to investigate and bring to justice individuals who commit genocide, crimes against humanity, war crimes and the crime of aggression, once its definition has been finalised.

Article 30

Freedom from State or other Interference in Any of the Above Rights

Since the Nuremberg Tribunal of 1945, the crime of aggression has been recognised as the supreme international offence, a crime against peace which often incites the most serious mass human rights violations, including genocide, war crimes and crimes against humanity. The statute of the International Criminal Court provides for criminal responsibility for the crime of aggression, which is generally understood to comprise planning, preparing, ordering, initiating or carrying out an armed attack or waging a war of aggression, in violation of international treaties. In such a scenario, only individuals in positions of leadership who order or actively participate in such acts of aggression could incur responsibility. However, there is still no consensus on a definition or legal precedent for individual criminal responsibility for acts of aggression, as opposed to wars of aggression. The crime of aggression will only be part of the Court's jurisdiction after a definition—sufficiently precise and clear to meet the high level of specificity required of criminal law—has been determined.

Some of the international crimes discussed but not included in the Rome Statute were the illicit traffic in narcotic drugs and substances, terrorism, and crimes against United Nations and associated personnel. As there is no unified international legal system for addressing the crimes of drug trafficking and terrorism, delegates agreed that these crimes could be more effectively investigated and prosecuted by national authorities under existing international cooperation agreements rather than by the International Criminal Court. This was also the rationale for not including crimes against United Nations personnel, which have been on the rise in recent years. Since 1992, almost 300 civilians have lost their lives in the service of the United Nations. Military peacekeeping personnel are also often the targets of assault, kidnapping and murder. This alarming situation prompted the General Assembly to adopt, in 1994, the Convention on the Safety of United Nations and Associated Personnel, which affirms individuals criminal responsibility for attacks against United Nations personnel.

Note: Human Rights: A United Nations Priority. Information current as of October 1998.

UNITED NATIONS LANDMARKS IN HUMAN RIGHTS: A BRIEF CHRONOLOGY

26 June 1945 — Signing of the *Charter of the United Nations* and the *Statute of the International Court of Justice*, in San Francisco.

21 June 1946 — The Economic and Social Council (ECOSOC) establishes the *Commission on Human Rights* and the *Commission on the Status of Women*.

9 December 1948 — The General Assembly adopts the *Convention on the Prevention and Punishment of the Crime of Genocide* (entered into force 1951).

10 December 1948 — The General Assembly adopts the *Universal Declaration of Human Rights*.

12 August 1949 — The Diplomatic Conference for the Establishment of International Conventions for the Protection of Victims of War adopts four *Geneva Conventions*, relating to the Amelioration of the Condition of Wounded and Sick Members of Armed Forces in the Field and at Sea, the Treatment of Prisoners of War and the Protection of Civilians in Wartime (into force 1950).

20 December 1952 — The General Assembly adopts the *Convention on the Political Rights of Women* (into force 1954).

1 August 1956 — ECOSOC calls for periodic reports (every three years) on human rights and studies of specific rights or groups of rights. This resolution represents the first call for reports from Member States, and was a precursor to the reporting requirements contained in the many subsequent human rights covenants.

20 November 1959 The General Assembly adopts the *Declaration of the Rights of the Child* (see also 20 November 1989).

21 December 1965 The General Assembly adopts the *International Convention on the Elimination of All Forms of Racial Discrimination* (into force 1969). This Convention provides for the establishment of the Committee on the Elimination of Racial Discrimination.

16 December 1966 The General Assembly adopts the *International Covenant on Economic, Social and Cultural rights* (into force 3 January 1976) and the *International Covenant on Civil and Political Rights* with an *Optional Protocol* (into force 23 March 1976). This Covenant provides for the establishment of the Human Rights Committee (see also 28 May 1985).

6 June 1967 ECOSOC adopts *resolution 1235 (XLII)*, authorising the Commission on Human Rights and the Subcommission on Prevention of Discrimination and Protection of Minorities to examine information relevant to gross violations of human rights and fundamental freedoms.

7 November 1967 The General Assembly adopts the *Declaration on the Elimination of Discrimination against Women*.

13 May 1968	The International Conference on Human Rights adopts the *Proclamation of Tehran.*
26 November 1968	The General Assembly adopts the *Convention on the Non-Applicability of Statutory Limitations to War Crimes against Humanity* (into force 1970).
11 December 1969	The General Assembly adopts the Declaration on Social Progress and Development.
30 November 1973	The General Assembly adopts the *International Convention on the Suppression and Punishment of the Crime of Apartheid* (into force 1976).
9 December 1975	The General Assembly adopts the *Declaration on the Protection of All Persons from Being Subjected to Torture and Other Cruel, Inhuman or Degrading Treatment or Punishment.*
23 March 1976	With entry into force of the *International Covenant on Civil and Political Rights* and the *International Covenant on Economic, Social and Cultural Rights*, 10 years after being originally opened for signature (see 16 December 1966), the *International Bill of Human Rights* becomes a reality (see also 10 December 1948).
18 December 1979	The General Assembly adopts the *Convention on the Elimination of All Forms of Discrimination against Women* (into force 1981). The Convention provides for the establishment of the Committee on the Elimination of Discrimination against Women.

25 November 1981	The General Assembly adopts the *Declaration on the Elimination of all Forms of Intolerance and of Discrimination Based on Religion or Belief.*
10 December 1984	The General Assembly adopts the *Convention against torture and Other Cruel, Inhuman or Degrading Treatment or Punishment* (into force 1987). The Convention provides for the establishment of the Committee against Torture.
28 May 1985	ECOSOC establishes the *Committee on Economic, Social and Cultural Rights*, responsible for monitoring the implementation of the *International Covenant on Economic, Social and Cultural Rights.*
4 December 1986	The General Assembly adopts the *Declaration on the Right to Development.*
9 December 1988	The General Assembly adopts the *Body of Principles for the Protection of All Persons under Any Form of Detention or Imprisonment.*
24 May 1989	ECOSOC adopts the *Principles on the Effective Prevention and Investigation of Extralegal, Arbitrary and Summary Executions.*
20 November 1989	The General Assembly adopts the *Convention on the Rights of the Child* (into force 1990). The Convention provides for the establishment of the Committee on the Rights of the Child.
18 December 1990	The General Assembly adopts the *International Convention on the*

	Protection of the Rights of All Migrant Workers and Members of their Families.
18 December 1992	The General Assembly adopts the *Declaration on the Rights of Persons Belonging to National or Ethnic, Religious and Linguistic Minorities.*
25 May 1993	The Security Council adopts resolution 827 (1993), establishing an *International Criminal Tribunal for the Prosecution of Persons Responsible for Serious Violations of International Humanitarian Law Committed in the Territory of the former Yoguslavia since 1991*, with its seat at The Hague in the Netherlands.
25 June 1993	The World Conference on Human Rights adopts the *Vienna Declaration and Programme of Action.*
20 December 1993	The General Assembly adopts resolution 48/141, establishing the post of *United Nations High Commissioner for Human Rights.*
5 April 1994	Mr. José Ayala Lasso of Ecuador assumes the post of first *United Nations High Commissioner for Human Rights.*
8 November 1994	The Security Council adopts resolution 955 (1994), establishing an *International Criminal Tribunal for the Prosecution of Persons Responsible for Genocide and Other Serious Crimes against Humanitarian Law Committed in Rwanda during 1994*, with its seat in Arusha, Tanzania.
23 December 1994	The General Assembly proclaims the *United Nations Decade for Human Rights Education (1995-2004).*

12 September 1997	Ms. Mary Robinson of Ireland becomes the second *United Nations High Commissioner for Human Rights.*
17 July 1998	The Diplomatic Conference of Plenipotentiaries adopts the *Rome Statute of the International Criminal Court*, establishing the International Criminal Court, with its seat at The Hague.

THE UNIVERSAL DECLARATION OF HUMAN RIGHTS: A SYNOPSIS

This abbreviated version of the 30 Articles of the Universal Declaration of Human Rights provides an overview of the principal rights and freedoms that are every person's birthright.

The first two articles are fundamental principles underlying all human rights. Articles 3 to 21 comprise civil and political rights. Articles 22 to 27 refer to economic, social and cultural rights. The last three articles provide a framework of solidarity safeguarding the universal enjoyment of all human rights.

Article 1	Right to freedom and equality in dignity and rights
Article 2	Freedom from discrimination
Article 3	Right to life, liberty and security of person
Article 4	Freedom from slavery and servitude
Article 5	Freedom from torture or degrading treatment
Article 6	Right to recognition as a person before the law
Article 7	Right to equal consideration before the law
Article 8	Right to remedy through a competent tribunal
Article 9	Freedom from arbitrary arrest or exile
Article 10	Right to a fair trial or public hearing

Article 11	Right to be considered innocent until proven guilty
Article 12	Freedom from interference with privacy, including home, family and correspondence
Article 13	Right to freedom of movement and residence in one's own country and to leave and return at will
Article 14	Right to asylum
Article 15	Right to a nationality and freedom to change it
Article 16	Right to marriage and protection of family
Article 17	Right to own property
Article 18	Freedom of belief and religion
Article 19	Freedom of opinion and information
Article 20	Right to peaceful assembly and association
Article 21	Right to participate in government and in free elections and to equal access to public service
Article 22	Right to social security
Article 23	Right to work and fair pay for work
Article 24	Right to rest and leisure
Article 25	Right to adequate standard of living for health and well-being
Article 26	Right to education
Article 27	Right to participate in the cultural life of the community
Article 28	Right to social order assuring human rights
Article 29	Responsibility to community essential to free and full development of the individual
Article 30	Freedom from State or other interference in any of the above rights

INTERNATIONAL HUMAN RIGHTS INSTRUMENTS

There are over 60 international human rights instruments today, and some are listed below. The core human rights treaties, which have established treaty bodies to monitor their implementation, are marked with an asterisk. Also listed is the year of adoption of a treaty and, where applicable, the year it entered into force and the current status of ratifications, as of August 1998.

Charter of the United Nations (1945)

International Bill of Human Rights

Universal Declaration of Human Rights (1948)

International Covenant on Economic, Social and Cultural Rights (adopted 1966, entry into force 1976, 137 ratifications)*

International Covenant on Civil and Political Rights (adopted 1966, entry into force 1976, 140 ratifications)*

First Optional Protocol to the International Covenant on Civil and Political Rights, allowing individuals to submit complaints to the Human Rights Committee (adopted 1966, entry into force 1976, 92 ratifications)

Second Optional Protocol to the International Covenant on Civil and Political Rights, aimed at the abolition of the death penalty (adopted 1989, entry into force 1991, 33 ratifications)

Prevention of Discrimination

Declaration on the Elimination of All Forms of Racial Discrimination (1963)

International Convention on the Elimination of All Forms of Racial Discrimination (1965, 1969, 150)*

International Convention on the Suppression and Punishment of the Crime of Apartheid (1973, 1976, 101)

Declaration on the Elimination of All Forms of Intolerance and of Discrimination Based on Religion or Belief (1981)

Declaration on the Rights of Persons Belonging to National or Ethnic, Religious and Linguistic Minorities (1992)

ILO Convention concerning Employment and Occupation Discrimination (1958, 1960)

UNESCO Convention against Discrimination in Education (1960)

UNESCO Declaration on Race and Racial Prejudice (1978)

Human Rights of Women

Convention on the Political Rights of Women (1952, 1954, 110)

Declaration on the Elimination of All Forms of discrimination against Women (1967)

Declaration on the Protection of Women and Children in Emergency and Armed Conflict (1974)

Convention on the Elimination of All Forms of Discrimination against Women (1979, 1981, 161)*

Declaration on the Elimination of Violence against Women (1993)

Rights of the Child

Declaration on the Rights of the Child (1959)

Declaration on the Protection of Women and Children in Emergency and Armed Conflict (1974)

Declaration on Social and Legal Principles relating to the Protection and Welfare of Children, with Special Reference to Foster Placement and Adoption Nationally and Internationally (1986)

Convention on the Rights of the Child (1989, 1990, 191)*

Human Rights in the Administration of Justice

Declaration on the Protection of All Persons from Being Subjected to Torture and Other Cruel, Inhuman or Degrading Treatment or Punishment (1975)

Convention against Torture and Other Cruel, Inhuman or Degrading Treating or Punishment (1984, 1987, 105)*

Basic Principles on the Independence of the Judiciary (1985)

Body of Principles for the Protection of All Persons under Any Form of Detention or Imprisonment (1988)

Principles on the Effective Prevention and Investigation of Extra-legal, Arbitrary and Summary Executions (1989)

Basic Principles for the Treatment of Prisoners (1990)

Declaration on the Protection of All Persons from Enforced Disappearances (1992)

Social Welfare, Progress and Development

Declaration on Social Progress and Development (1969)

Declaration on the Rights of Mentally Retarded Persons (1971)

Universal Declaration on the Eradication of Hunger and Malnutrition (1974)

Declaration on the Use of Scientific and Technological Progress in the Interests of Peace and for the Benefit of Mankind (1975)

Declaration on the Rights of Disabled Persons (1975)

Declaration on the Right of Peoples to Peace (1984)

Declaration on the Right to Development (1986)

International Convention on the Protection of the Rights of All Migrant Workers and Members of Their Families (1990)

Slavery, Servitude, Forced Labour and similar Institutions and Practices

Slavery Convention (1926, 1927, 40)

Convention for the Suppression of the Traffic in Persons and of the Exploitation of the Prostitution of Others (1949, 1951, 72)

Protocol amending the Slavery Convention (1953, 1953, 59)

Supplementary Convention on the Abolition of Slavery, the Slave Trade, and Institutions and Practices Similar to Slavery (1956, 1957, 117)

War Crimes and Crimes against Humanity, including genocide

Convention on the Prevention and Punishment of the Crime of Genocide (1948, 1951, 125)

Convention on the Non-Applicability of Statutory Limitations to War Crimes and Crimes against Humanity (1968, 1970, 43)

Principles of international cooperation in the detection, arrest, extradition and punishment of persons guilty of war crimes and crimes against humanity (1973)

Humanitarian Law

Geneva Convention for the Amelioration of the Condition of the Wounded and Sick in Armed Forces in the Field (1949, 1950)

Geneva Convention for the Amelioration of the Condition of Wounded, Sick and Shipwrecked Members of Armed forces at Sea (1949, 1950)

Geneva Convention relative to the Treatment of Prisoners of War (1949, 1950)

Geneva Convention relative to the Protection of Civilian Persons in Time of War (1949, 1950)

Protocol Additional to the Geneva Conventions of 12 August 1949, and relating to the Protection of Victims of International Armed Conflicts (Protocol I) (1977, 1979)

Protocol Additional to the Geneva Conventions of 12 August 1949, and relating to the Protection of Victims of Non-International Armed Conflicts (Protocol II) (1977, 1978)

Nationality, Statelessness, Asylum and Refugees

Convention relating to the Status of Refugees (1951, 1954, 132)

Convention relating to the Status of Stateless Persons (1954, 1960, 44)

Convention on the Nationality of Married Women (1957, 1958, 66)

Protocol relating to the Status of Refugees (1966, 1967, 132)

Declaration on Territorial Asylum (1967)

Declaration on the Human Rights of Individuals Who Are Not Nationals of the Country in Which They Live (1985)

Right to Self-Determination

Declaration on the Granting of Independence to colonial Countries and Peoples (1960)

Freedom of Association

ILO Convention on Freedom of Association and Protection of the Right to Organise (1948, 1950)

ILO Convention on the Right to Organise and Collective Bargaining (1949, 1951)

Employment

ILO Convention concerning the Promotion of Collective Bargaining (1981, 1983)

ILO Convention concerning Employment Promotion and Protection against Unemployment (1988, 1991)

ILO Convention concerning Indigenous and Tribal Peoples in Independent Countries (1989, 1991)

Marriage, Family and Youth

Convention on Consent to Marriage, Minimum Age for Marriage and Registration of Marriages (1962, 1964, 47)

Right to Enjoy Culture, International Cultural Development and Cooperation

Declaration of the Principles of International Cultural Co-operation (1966)

OFFICE OF THE UNITED NATIONS HIGH COMMISSIONER FOR HUMAN RIGHTS

In 1997, the human rights programme of the United Nations was fundamentally restructured in order to strengthen its impact on the coordination of human rights activities throughout the system. The Secretary-General merged the High Commissioner's Office and the former Centre for Human Rights into a single human rights programme, the Office of the United Nations High Commissioner for Human Rights.

Three branches of the High Commissioner's Office now perform the functional activities of the former Centre for Human Rights: the Research and Right to Development Branch, the Support Services Branch and the Activities and Programmes Branch.

The Research and Right to Development Branch is involved in all activities related to the promotion and protection of the right to development, in particular by supporting the working groups on the realisation of the right to development, and is also responsible for carrying out research projects. It also supports all thematic mandates and the work of the Subcommission on Prevention of Discrimination and Protection of Minorities.

The Support Services Branch serves as a secretariat to the six treaty bodies, the voluntary funds and to the Commission on Human Rights and its subsidiary bodies. It also processes the hundreds of thousands of complaints from individuals addressed to the United Nations each year.

The Activities and Programmes Branch coordinates all Advisory Services and Technical Cooperation Projects and the human rights field offices worldwide. It manages the Voluntary Funds for Advisory Services and Technical Cooperation Projects and for Field Presences, and is responsible for implementing the Plan of Action for the Decade for Human Rights Education. The Branch provides support to the Special Rapporteurs of the Commission on Human Rights, and maintains country desk offices dealing with the human rights situation in specific countries.

UNITED NATIONS HUMAN RIGHTS MONITORING MECHANISMS

At the heart of the United Nations monitoring system are the two types of human rights monitoring mechanisms. The so-called conventional mechanisms refer to the specific committees formally established through the principal international human rights treaties. These "treaty bodies" monitor the implementation of the individual conventions by the State parties.

Over the years, the United Nations has also developed an independent and ad hoc system of fact-finding outside the treaty framework, which is referred to as extra-conventional mechanisms or "special procedures". Independent experts report in their personal capacity as special rapporteurs or as members of working groups.

Treaty Bodies (Conventional Mechanisms)

Treaty bodies have been set up for the six core United Nations human rights treaties to monitor States parties' efforts to implement the provisions of the international instruments.

The Human Rights Committee (HRC) monitors the implementation of the International Covenant on civil and Political Rights. Composed of 18 independent experts of recognised competence in the field of human rights, the Committee was established when the Covenant entered into force in 1976. The First, Optional Protocol, which entered into force together with the Covenant, authorises the Committee to consider also allegations from individuals concerning violations of their civil and political rights. The Committee is also concerned with the Second Optional Protocol on the Abolition of the Death Penalty.

The Committee on Economic, Social and Cultural Rights (CESCR) monitors the International Covenant on Economic, Social and Cultural Rights. Composed on 18 internationally recognised independent experts in the relevant fields, the Committee was established by the Economic and Social Council in 1985, nine years after the Covenant entered into force. Unlike the other committees, whose members are elected by the States parties to the respective convention and report to the General Assembly, the members of the Committee on Economic, Social and Cultural Rights are elected by ECOSOC, to which they report.

The Committee on the Elimination of Racial Discrimination (CERD) monitors the implementation of the International Convention on the Elimination of All Forms of Racial Discrimination. Composed of 18 independent experts, the Committee began its work when the Convention entered into force in 1969 and is the oldest treaty body.

The Committee on the Elimination of Discrimination against Women (CEDAW), composed of 23 independent experts, has monitored the Convention on the Elimination of All Forms of Discrimination against Women since 1981.

The Committee against Torture (CAT) monitors the Convention against Torture and Other Cruel, Inhuman or Degrading Treatment or Punishment. Composed of 10 independent experts, the Committee was established in 1987.

The Committee on the Rights of the Child (CRC), composed of 10 independent experts, has monitored the Convention on the Rights of the Child since 1991.

Special Procedures of the Commission on Human Rights (Extra-Conventional Mechanisms)

The ad hoc nature of the special procedures of the Commission on Human Rights allows for a more flexible response to serious human rights violations than the treaty bodies. Experts entrusted with special human rights mandates act in their personal capacity and are variously designated as Special Rapporteur, Representative, Independent Expert or, when several experts share a mandate, Working Group. They examine, monitor and publicly report to the Commission either on human rights situations in specific countries and territories or on global phenomena that cause serious human rights violations worldwide. Certain special mandates are also entrusted to the Secretary-General or his Special Representatives. While never originally conceived as a system, the nearly 50 country and thematic mechanisms that have been established thus far clearly constitute and function as an effective system of human rights protection.

Country Mechanisms

Currently, some 20 mandates monitor the human rights situation in specific countries, including Afghanistan, Burundi, Cambodia, the Democratic Republic of the Congo (formerly Zaire), Equatorial Guinea, Haiti, the Islamic Republic of Iran, Iraq, Myanmar, Nigeria, Rwanda, Somalia, Sudan and the former Yugoslavia.

The General Assembly has established a Special Committee to Investigate Israeli Practices Affecting the Human Rights of the Palestinian People and Other Arabs of the Occupied Territories.

Thematic Mechanisms

The General Assembly has established a Special Representative of the Secretary-General for Children in Armed Conflict.

The Commission on Human Rights has established a Special Representative of the Secretary-General on Internally Displaced Persons and has created a number of important thematic mandates on:

Arbitrary detention

Contemporary forms of racism, racial discrimination, xenophobia, and related intolerance

Effects of foreign debt on the full enjoyment of economic, social and cultural rights

Effects of illicit dumping of toxic wastes and dangerous products on the enjoyment of human rights

Enforced or involuntary disappearances

Extrajudicial, summary or arbitrary executions

Freedom of opinion and expression

Human rights and extreme poverty

Independence of judges and lawyers

Religious intolerance

Right to development

Right to education

Sale of children, child prostitution and child pornography

Structural adjustment policies

Torture

Use of mercenaries and the right of peoples to self-determination

Violence against women

The Subcommission on Prevention of Discrimination and Protection of Minorities has also established a number of thematic mechanisms.

There are Working Groups on:

Communications (the 1503 Procedure reviewing individual complaints)

Contemporary forms of slavery

Indigenous populations

Minorities

The Subcommission has also appointed Special Rapporteurs and Independent Experts to conduct studies, including

Impunity concerning economic, social and cultural rights

Impunity concerning civil and political rights

Human rights dimension of population transfer

Human rights and income distribution

Traditional practices affecting the health of women and the girl child

Systematic rape and sexual slavery during armed conflict

Treaties, agreements and other arrangements between States and indigenous populations

Human rights and states of emergency

Privatisation of prisons

Freedom of movement

Human rights and terrorism

Human rights and scientific progress

Thematic mandates are also entrusted to the Secretary-General, at the level of either the Commission on Human Rights or the Subcommission, including

Human rights in the Context of HIV/AIDS

Human rights and forensic science

Human rights and mass exoduses

Human rights and terrorism

Rape and abuse of women in the areas of armed conflict in the former Yugoslavia

Reprisals against persons cooperating with United Nations human rights bodies